Graphology and the Psychology of Handwriting

Graphology and the Psychology of Handwriting

by

JUNE E. DOWNEY

Professor of Psychology University of Wyoming

GYAN

Published by

GYAN

Gyan Publishing House
5, Ansari Road
Daryaganj, New Delhi-110002
Phone: 011-47034999, 9811692060
E-mail: books@gyanbooks.com

Distribution Network
gyanbooks.com
India, USA, Canada, UK, Australia, France

ISBN : 978-81-212-2315-7 (PB)
First Published, 1919

2nd Impression 2021

Printed at: Gyan Press, Delhi.

Graphology and the Psychology of Handwriting
Author: June E. Downey

Graphology and the Psychology of Handwriting

By

JUNE E. DOWNEY

Professor of Psychology, University of Wyoming

BALTIMORE

WARWICK & YORK, Inc.

1919

To

William O. Owen

In recognition of his devotion

To

Truth as an Ideal

CONTENTS

PART I.

PART II. EXPERIMENTAL.

PREFACE

The following studies are designed to canvass the possibility of a scientific characterological utilization of handwriting. Their main purpose is one of orientation, preliminary to an attempt to use graphic activity in tests of temperamental or character traits, tests which are now in process of standardization.

The discussion falls into two parts. Part I consists mainly of a critical comparison of graphological contentions and the outcome of modern scientific investigations of handwriting. Part II reports a number of experimental studies, designed largely to try out various methods of approach. Free use is made of results from other experimental investigations by myself which have been previously reported. The chapter on "Disguised Handwriting" is reprinted, with a few minor additions, from the Journal of Applied Psychology.

The "Graphological Study of the Handwriting of Psychologists" was made possible through the generous assistance of those psychologists who furnished me with the material necessary for a characterological rating. In the study on "Intra-Individual Variability," I am greatly indebted to John E. Anderson for faithful coöperation; and in other studies I have had the kind assistance of my pupils and colleagues at the University of Wyoming. I take this opportunity of expressing to all who have aided me my heartiest thanks.

JUNE E. DOWNEY.

University of Wyoming, August, 1918.

Part I

CHAPTER I.

INTRODUCTION.

The present day preoccupation with applied and, particularly, with vocational psychology has revived an interest in attempts to analyze character by means of physical traits or objective products. We have, for example, systems of character analysis based upon so-called fundamental physical variables such as pigmentation, form, size, structure, and expression. Graphology as an alleged science of psychodiagnosis utilizes a particular form of expression, namely, handwriting. Graphology as so defined should, however, be discriminated from the graphology which is a study of graphic signs of service in the identification of writing. Both uses of the word are current today; in our present discussion we are mainly interested in the former.

It has been assumed by many scientific workers that graphology as a system of character diagnosis is on a level with other pseudo-sciences which look for a facile interpretation of one's mental make-up from a reading of the lines in the palm of the hand or the bumps on the head. And, in fact, certain extravagant claims of certain ambitious graphologists relative to the possibility of determining the color of a writer's eyes or the shape of his nose or the elasticity of his bank-account from his chirographic style justify a healthy incredulity. The best graphologists show, however, a caution and conservatism in interpretation that wins in a measure the reader's confidence and a desire to hear what those of best repute have to say in defense of their art.

So far as the details of graphological diagnosis go one may, indeed, be exceedingly sceptical and yet unwilling to dismiss the whole matter on the ground that graphology is on a par with palmistry, phrenology, or astrology. However mistaken and overly optimistic graphologists may have been; however obviously inadequate their control of observations, the precipitate from the extensive study of such men as Preyer, Crépieux-Jamin, Meyer, Schneidemühl, and Klages certainly deserves respectful consideration. Moreover, on the general ground of intimate relationship between consciousness and motor expression, the graphic pattern which we call handwriting individuality demands careful scrutiny. Possibly the determinants of handwriting individuality may be wholly external to the individual's psychic make-up, but the statement should at least be accompanied by an interrogation point. A more conservative position grants the possibility at some future day of utilizing handwriting in psychodiagnosis but would defer such an attempt until a more perfect technique has been acquired by psychologists for analysis of the grapho-motor process and the graphic product. The wisdom of this position is evident but an endeavor to try out immediately certain graphological principles seems justifiable for the following reason.

Mental testing which is opening out into such tremendous possibilities with reference to the analysis of the intelligence make-up is still baffled by the problem of diagnostic tests for character and temperamental traits. But the need of such tests is as obvious as difficulties in the way of getting them are great. Especially necessary in vocational selection is a determination of character qualifications. Two individuals of equally keen intelligence may be very unequally fitted for the same position by reason of difference in degree of persistence, energy, ambition, self-confidence and the like. After a certain level of intelligence is attained, barring cases of exceptional ability, success in life would seem to be dictated more largely by temperamental qualities than by mentality status. The need for diagnostic tests of such qualities therefore renders unnecessary any extensive apology for excursions even into debatable territory. The slightest chance of stumbling upon a useful suggestion of procedure justifies such an excursion.

But only those readers who have attempted to work through it are aware how voluminous is the literature of graphology. This literature is found mainly in the French and German languages. Discussions of graphology by English writers suffer greatly by comparison, so much more subtle, discriminating, and scholarly are the former. A somewhat close reading of a number of these works has convinced me that a summary of the points of view involved might be profitably undertaken. If nothing more, it may stimulate the psychology of handwriting to novel methods of approach.

In my survey of graphological doctrine I have followed, largely, a comparative treatment. I have sought, that is, to present graphological material in light of the perspective furnished by the modern scientific study of handwriting. Such study has pursued several differing lines of interest, very differently motivated. A word as to each will serve to map out our territory.

1. The most scientific study of handwriting has centered its interest in a delicate analysis of the graphic movements as a form of motor reaction. Such investigators have developed and are perfecting an elaborate instrumental technique. One recalls in this connection the fine work of Gross, Diehl, Meumann, Freeman and others.

2. Much less controlled and objective in its methods but valuable as an attempt to approach the analysis from another angle are attempts to determine certain mental factors that condition handwriting; the study, for example, of the imaginal and sensational control processes (Downey) or the factor of unconscious imitation (Starch).

3. A third investigation, motivated primarily by pedagogical interests, has served to establish definite standards for the evaluation of writing speed, quality and legibility. Various scales of evaluation of graphic products have been put to extensive use, among them the widely known scales of Ayers and Thorndike.

4. Under pressure of practical need for accurate identification of handwriting for legal purposes, both civil and criminal, the handwriting experts have given us detailed analyses of the effect upon penmanship of writing systems and writing apparatus. They have stimulated discussions of the limits of variability and of disguise in the hands of individuals and have adopted a procedural technique that offers many a suggestion to the student of other aspects of the general problem. Particularly stimulating is the account by Osborn of the utilization by the expert of the most modern of mechanical appliances such as the document microscope, the enlarged photograph, and delicate scales for determination of line-width, degree of curvature of connecting lines and similar graphic details.

5. Very greatly in contrast to the regulated analysis of the legal expert are the descriptions of pathological writing furnished us by psychiatrists. Yet pathological writing affords, as we shall see, a unique method of checking up conclusions reached by other forms of procedure.

6. Lastly, we may list a line of investigation somewhat difficult to characterize. It consists in the utilization of writing as a material which may be employed in discovering certain types of perceptual and judgmental reaction. Strictly speaking our interest in this connection is not in the psychology of writing, as such, but in the psychology of the observer of graphic products. This latter aspect of the situation is implicit in graphology in so far as the graphologist gives evidence of virtuosity in his handling of graphic material. Binet's investigation of the graphologist approached the subject from this angle. Psychological investigation makes a similar approach in utilizing handwriting as a material for study of the subjective judgment in tracing family resemblances, and in training the expert judge of handwriting for school systems. The insistence by Osborn that extreme blindness to graphic form on the part of the presiding judge may seriously handicap presentation of evidence in the courts also stresses the significance of the sub-

jective factor in the applied psychology of handwriting.

Our general plan of procedure may now be outlined. The first part of this little volume proposes to discuss, with the critical background furnished by the specific investigations listed above in addition to general psychological theory, the following topics:

1. The general concepts upon which the graphologists build their elaborate structure.

2. The methods they have utilized in their endeavor to correlate particular graphic with particular mental or temperamental traits.

3. The significance of certain graphic elements as determined by graphology and by psychology.

The second part of the book will be devoted to reports on experimental investigation of a few specific graphological assumptions. Since the question of method of attack will, necessarily, be in the foreground, meagre positive results may be anticipated. Whatever positive conclusions are suggested will encourage us in our search for diagnostic material. The particular problems we shall attack in this part include handwriting disguise as basal to all efforts to discriminate between the spontaneous and the controlled hand; intra-individual variability; graphic individuality; and, lastly, a graphological reading of a collection of hands checked by a characterological rating obtained by a modified form of the order of merit method.

CHAPTER II.

THE BASAL CONCEPTS OF GRAPHOLOGY.

From my reading of graphological literature, five concepts emerge as essential to an understanding of the general assumptions. These concepts may be listed as follows: (1) Handwriting as a form of emotional or dramatic expression; (2) Graphic individuality as an outcome of central factors; (3) The limits of voluntary control and its significance for psychodiagnosis from written products; (4) The range and significance of graphic variability; and (5) The conception of the graphological signs and of the graphological portrait. Let us discuss briefly what is involved in each of these concepts.

1. *Handwriting as a form of Dramatic Expression.*

A general presupposition of graphology is that all movement has dramatic nuance and mirrors temperamental tendencies. Writing is described as an expressive movement on a par with gesture and emotional attitude. The French characterization of writing as composed of "petits gestes" conveys distinctly the point of view involved.

It may be said that this fundamental conception, even if true, is too general to be of much value. A serviceable application demands a definite comprehension of the principles underlying emotional and dramatic expression and its application to a series of abbreviated movements that are primarily constrained by the demands of social communication to the production of stereotyped signs that may vary only within certain prescribed limits. At best we have a baffling entangling of external and internal factors. Training, practice, convention "rigidify" the petit gesture. Yet, of course, all emotional expression both yields to and yet moulds conventional requirements, witness such forms as tone of voice, facial accents, bodily postures. How far, in fact, emotional attitudes are an outcome of conventionalized and traditional expression, how far dominated by racially ingrained patterns is itself a problem.

We shall have occasion to consider this question at closer quarters when reviewing the graphic signs that are selected as significant of emotional tendencies. Certainly, the broad classification of outgoing movements (eccentric) and movements of withdrawal (concentric) as characterizing respectively attitudes of aggression and of defense cannot sustain too great a weight. The situation will be canvassed more specifically when we come to deal with variations in Slant and Alignment, which are thought to carry emotional implications.

2. *The Central Factor in Handwriting Individuality.*

The existence of graphic individuality, often of a very pronounced type, will hardly be questioned. Its explanation is, however, open to discussion. Is individuality in handwriting a product of objective factors only? Or in despite of these does writing assume a specific character?

Perhaps the cleanest-cut treatment of handwriting individuality, although not necessarily the most convincing, is that furnished by the practical expert. It is of course his contention that no two hands are ever precisely identical; he is willing to stake his professional reputation upon the possibility of handwriting identification but he is apt to add that the individuality with which he deals is an outcome of the multiplicity of factors involved. Graphic individuality is acquired; its origin is to be sought in the system learned in school, in acquired habits of arm, wrist and finger movement, in the kind of writing apparatus that is utilized, in the amount of practice, in professional requirements, social imitation and the like. On a low basis of calculation as to possible variations in writing characters which have been determined by careful analysis, Osborn tells us that "the mathematical probability of two complete handwritings being identical is one in something more than sixty-eight trillions." **(36:233)**

The graphologists, on the other hand, assume that the individual stamp of penmanship is a matter largely of central origin. "Handscript" is, essentially, "Hirnschrift." As evidence of this they emphasize an observation frequently found in the literature of the subject that the writing of a given individual may be variously produced so far as musculature is concerned and still bear the individual stamp. We are told specifically that the foot-writing and the mouth-writing of a given individual resemble his hand-writing. (**39:37**) It is, moreover, a matter of general observation that one's free arm, magnified writing on the blackboard resembles one's finer pen-script executed perhaps with delicate finger movement.

The presence of central factors could not, of course, be cited as decisive so far as significance of graphic individuality is concerned. Objective conditions might leave a deposit of memory images of design and proportion of letters and the like which might well function in spite of shift in peripheral musculature or writing apparatus. But, obviously, the graphologist must mean something more than this. His conception of graphic style carries implications of the same stamp being impressed upon other movements executed by the individual in which there could be no question of the operation of specific graphic habits. He has, indeed, claimed that a similarity exists between a man's handwriting and the manner in which he walks or gesticulates; he has asserted that the pencraft of the painter mirrors the peculiar distinction that marks the sweep of his brush across the canvas.

I know of no controlled observations supporting such statements. Obviously there must be a wide range for error if such conclusions are based merely upon casual observations that are motivated by definite expectation and interest. In the second part of the book I shall report an attempt to test the assertion of the existence of individual motor patterns which stamp gesture and walk and posture as well as handwriting.

Psychologists who have made a special study of writing movements have had little to say of graphic individuality. Hirt(**23a:386**) speaks of unknown biological laws which are basal to handwriting individuality. Meumann holds, "It is the nature of innervations coming from the cerebral cortex, the form and extent to which they are synthesized, that is the main determinant of the character of the writing." **(32:337)**

Movement-individuality is probably a product of many different factors more or less fundamental to personality as a whole. Such, for example, are sensory predispositions, motor skill, degree of unidextrality and the like. Many of these contributing factors might well be discussed in detail but since individuality is a function of the complex as a whole rather than that of the elements as elements we may postpone certain observations until later. Series of samples showing the genetic development of hands would be of very great value in helping us to analyze the appearance and the consistency of graphic individuality. The great individual variation in the time at which handwriting sets or matures with a consequent fixation of "style" is one of the most interesting aspects of writing with which I am acquainted. Time of fixation appears in many instances to be a family trait and opens up the question of the possibility of innate and very fundamental tendencies reflected in the existence of family hands unless, of course, the family type be wholly the product of social and educational environment. Personally, I am convinced that family resemblance in chirography is not to be explained on the basis of similarity in teaching and social models. Nor indeed do I find its most impressive aspect in similarity in graphic details such as design of letters but rather in the appearance of general motor patterns, a fluidity or rigidity of movement, an inflection of manner that seems to lie back of the assumed features. Hirt's observations on this point are of particular value and his interesting citation of his own case carries considerable weight in favor of a heritable factor being involved in the situation

(**23a:386**). My own collection of cases carries the same import. (**14b**) While Thorndike on the assumption of a native factor has utilized the resemblance between the handwriting of twins as a means of getting a scale of unintentional resemblance. (**46b**) More recently still Starch has reported a correlation of .72 for speed of writing in a group of eighteen pairs of adult siblings, and a correlation of .46 for quality of writing. (**43b**)

3. *Control in Handwriting.*

In a sense the concept of voluntary control is the crucial one in graphology. Graphologists in accepting a specimen demand that it be a "bona fide" article. They refuse to handle what they call calligraphic or purely conventional hands—hands that lack individuality. They would seem to recognize the possibility of writing from which all individuality has been squeezed by pressure of professional necessity or by need for disguise. What it sought is a handwriting specimen in which the individual gives way to natural impulses of expression. They prefer for their purposes the free writing which one addresses to one's self in rapid note-taking or the writing in informal letters to intimates rather than the chirography on stilts which one assumes to impress another or for formal examination purposes.

That the limit of control is the crucial point in handwriting identification, has been clearly seen by the legal experts. Schneikert (**41**), for example, in planning for the Berlin police system a method of classification of the handwriting of criminals for purposes of identification bases his general scheme on the elements in writing that may be easily disguised or the reverse. Such graphic characteristics as size, slant, form of letters are easily modified at will; while relative proportion between one and two or three space letters, continuity of writing, mannerisms in dotting the i, etc., remain relatively constant even in an attempt to disguise writ-

:ral, the success of the legal expert depends upon edge of where to examine writing with the expectation of seeing the mask dropped. The most careful disguise lets light through at some point. Some trick in making a comma, or crossing the "t" may give away the secret. Furthermore, only the expert is aware of the significance of what we may call graphic inconsistencies, the appearance, for instance, of an alien letter-form in a writing of a particular type. Almost supernormal control is involved in inhibition of the numerous habits that have been evolved in the course of learning to write. Moreover, this excessive control manifests itself in the appearance in such artificial writing of numerous evidences of writing inhibition, hesitations, and retouching of letters. Often the flowing writing movement is replaced by a slow drawing movement which in itself is indicative of a high degree of voluntary control or effort.

So much we learn from the legal expert. The experimental graphologist has not been slow to utilize this conception of control in his study of writing-types.

Klages (**26b**) discussing the meaning and limitations of the concept of handwriting as a type of individual behavior states that one should attempt to diagnose character from writing only after a thoroughgoing effort to classify a particular writing with reference to the amount of control exercised in the writing-act. He classifies writing as either (1) artificial or (2) natural. Artificial writing includes disguised, calligraphic, and ornamental writing. Under natural or spontaneous writing we get (a) a more controlled and (b) a more involuntary type of writing. Control in writing may arise either from mastery of impulse or from excessive inhibition. Involuntary or uncontrolled writing also shows variations dependent upon acquired traits. It is shown, however, that the concept of an acquired handwriting absolutely inexpressive of the writer's organization is but a limiting notion. Power of disguise or a high degree of sustained control are themselves significant traits.

4. *Variability.*

The concept of variability is allied to that of control. It may be considered from two standpoints, first, that of specific variability in the writing of different persons under set conditions; and, secondly, range of variability in the writing of a particular individual.

The extent and quality of graphic variations that may be anticipated under given conditions such as emotional disturbance, nervous disease and the like or those that are dependent upon age, sex, and profession will be rehearsed in other connections. We may confine ourselves here to consideration of variability in the writing of a given individual. Is this variability so great as to prohibit all utilization of writing in character-study?

Absolute invariability in graphic products is, of course, unthinkable. One of the most suspicious signs of a forgery by tracery consists in an exact reproduction of a signature. The existence of two absolutely identical natural autographs is an impossibility, the experts tell us. Their comparisons involve of course microscopic measurements and not the mere testimony of the bare eye. But granting a variable element in all graphic expression, is it so extreme as to lead us to conclude that writing individuality is too fluid a thing to have diagnostic significance?

Such a question could be answered only by an estimation of the actual extent of variability found in the writing of a given reagent under cited conditions.. In the hope of getting some exact determination of the range of variability I gathered the material and made the measurements reported in one of the studies in Part II. The range of variability was found to be pretty extreme but without loss of individuality. Variability in particular graphic signs and the interpretation of the significance of such specific variation is another matter.

In any case, the common exclamation of laymen, "I never write twice alike," is subject to big discount. The similarity in writings that may have elicted such a comment—one I have heard again and again—may be so striking as to lead the experimenter to wonder at the blindness of the person in question. Undoubtedly, however, one is more sensitive to minor variations in one's own writing or in that of members of one's household than to variation in that of acquaintances, just as most of us are less ready than strangers to see resemblances in the family circle.

It should be noted at this point that the writing-expert is accustomed to find graphic variability limited by the writing habits which are a product of the kind of movement and writing-systems learned and the amount of practice or graphic expertness. Variability is introduced by objective factors such, for example, as the haste or leisure with which one writes, the quality of pen, paper, and ink, the innumerable chance factors that have a casual and not a causal significance.

The best graphologists are aware of such factors conditioning the appearance of a handwriting under examination. They demand many specimens of a given writing produced under varying conditions.. They refuse, frequently, to attempt interpretation of unaccustomed, official, clerical, or so-called calligraphic writing. They ask for running writing produced under natural conditions of interest in the content.

5. *The Theory of Signs; The Graphological Portrait.*

In organizing their systems and presenting a technique of procedure, graphologists are wont to list so-called graphological signs or elements together with an interpretation of their significance. Variations occur, of course, in the various presentations. Under some form, however, all writers upon the subject deal with such graphic elements as size, alignment, slant, degree of continuity, proportion and the like. Usually a multiplicity of causes for the same effect is canvassed.

The mechanical aspect of much of the work with "signs" has been definitely criticized and in practice the graphologists modify their analytic procedure by an attempt to interpret each detail in the light of the setting in which it occurs. In the conception of the graphological portrait, the synthetic function of graphology is stressed at expense of the analytic. The real measure of a graphologist's expertness consists in his ability to interpret graphic signs in their relation to one another and to the whole complex in which they occur. He must synthesize a multiplicity of details, reconcile opposing symptoms and succeed in locating the central characteristic that furnishes the key to an understanding of the organization of diverse traits into a unique personality.

A balancing process somewhat similar is urged by Dr. Blackford (**5**) upon those who would use successfully her system of character-analysis. It is not sufficient to list for any individual the fundamental physical variables, color, size, texture, form and the like. One must be skilled in determining how one characteristic modifies another in the way of accentuation or neutralization; as, for instance, the degree to which convexity of form annuls brunette coloring. One must discover a unity back of apparent contradictions.

At this point scientific analysis is abandoned for artistic creation. Just as little as a cataloguing of psycho-physical traits can give us the living personalities of fiction and drama can a tabular summary of graphic characteristics and their significance give us the graphological portrait.

Two very interesting problems are involved in this conception. First, to what extent, if any, will science ever succeed in capturing the inmost citadel of personality? And, secondly, can it force its way in by any such a tour de force as that of the trained intuitions of the graphologist or of the physiognomist or other student of expression?

The attempt of the psychologist to penetrate the secrets of character-organization is evident in his recent torturing of the instinctive life in his search for an all-sufficient principle of interpretation. That he has made valuable discoveries must be conceded so far as his skill in twitching out of the pattern certain threads is in question. His success at synthesis is less evident as shown by the sense of violated personality that his analyses leave with us in contrast to our acquiescence in the portrayal of the same individuality by the great dramatist or fictionist. Quite probably it is a mistake to confuse the functions of science and art. So far as theoretical psychology is concerned her function may well be limited to furnishing a technique for character-analysis with, at most, a cataloguing of certain temperamental and character patterns and correlational formulae. But applied psychology will probably not content itself with bare formulae; it will develop the expert diagnostician whose advise anent matters of vocational pursuits or mental hygiene will be very definitely controlled by the results of a clinical examination conducted by himself or his specialists but will involve further a fusion in the white light of character-divination. The expert medical diagnostician also posseses this synthetic activity to a high degree we are told. How far such a gift is the outcome of original genius, how far the result of previous analysis and rich experience it is impossible to say in our present ignorance. It brings us face to face with many curious problems that are inherent in the concepts of "Intuition" and "Automatic Acitivity" and with certain aspects of the analytic versus the synthetic method of handling material to which we shall return in a later discussion.

The answer to our second question, the adequacy of certain forms of comprehensive character diagnosis, is very simple. They have not as yet been able to substantiate their claims. We hear of skilled readers of the human countenance but where may one find reported a controlled test of their actual proficiency? Business psychology is, however, envisaging this problem at close quarters and it may discover in time a specialized ability for speedy and accurate estimate of human nature on the bases of physical form and expression but from present indications it appears more likely to recommend instead a complete substitution of standardized mental tests as more accurate than the immediate judgment of the most experienced judge of human nature.

The proficiency of professional graphologists in delineation of the graphological portrait can be estimated only by controlled tests. It is not easy to win the consent of a professional to the precautions that are necessary. Binet (**3c**), however, succeeded in gaining the confidence of the French graphologists but in order to estimate their success or failure in numerical form he was compelled to limit his test to investigation of more or less mutilated aspects of character-reading, namely the determination of sex, age, and comparative intelligence and morality from chirography. The specific results of Binet's investigations we shall have occasion to refer to as the discussion develops. Suffice it to say here that Binet concluded that although there was something of truth in graphology as practiced by his collaborators, there was also much gross error and uncertainty. Graphology he thought might, however, be a science of the future. Quite possibly handwriting may be utilized in character diagnosis but in a much more modest form than is implied in the notion of the graphological portrait.

CHAPTER III.

GRAPHOLOGICAL METHODS.

In connection with a detailed discussion of the correlation of mental traits with specific graphic signs, we shall have occasion to handle this topic with some care. In this chapter let us confine ourselves to general observations.

In reading graphological literature I have frequently asked myself what evidence could be cited for particular conclusions and, frequently, I have been unable to put my finger on the method by which the conclusion was reached. It is, in fact, a rather difficult matter classifying or characterizing the kinds of evidence utilized. They are implicit rather than explicit in the graphological treatment, as is usually the case when a complex material is handled by a method of procedure that may be described as intuitive rather than analytical, artistic rather than scientific. An exhaustive study of the logic of graphology would probably repay the investigator. I shall, however, content myself with characterization of what I take to be the chief methods utilized by graphologists, namely, (1)) The Method of Analogy; (2) The Deduction of certain conclusions from general Psychological Principles; (3) The Inductive Method of Empirical Observation and of Comparative Study of Group and Individual Variation; (4) The Intuitional Procedure; (5) Experimental Graphology; (6) Pathological Writing.

In actual procedure these different methods are pretty thoroughly intertwined and some violence is done to a particular treatment by twitching them apart. Nevertheless, some schematism is necessary.

1. *The Method of Analogy.*

In breaking ground in every line of human endeavor recourse to analogy is evident. In primitive mental life we find rich material for study of the way in which many curious practices may grow up through associations by similarity. Wells, (note) quoting Josiah Moses, cites the following examples. "Bloodroot, on account of its red juice, is good for the blood; liverwort, having a leaf like the liver, cures disease of the liver—" etc. These early analogies impress us as crude in the extreme and amusing as well as inconsequential. Yet organization of experience is to a great degree dependent upon fusion of experiences on the basis of rough and, at first, superficial likenesses. And in more refined forms this method continues to dominate thought.

My general impression from reading graphological literature was that considerable appeal was made to very superficial analogies. But I do not find that I can list many such associations. I have the feeling, however, that the attribution of a given significance to a certain graphic sign was often based originally on a facile use of association by similiarity and that the psychological grounding is an afterthought. Purely analogical, I should say, is the deduction of the serpent-temperament—that of the diplomat (!)—from sinuous alignment or undulant bar of the t; and the paralleling of graphic and mental continuity, so that the quality of coherent thought is ascribed to the writer of a connected hand, and intermittent flashes of inspiration credited to him who indulges in frequent breaks in graphic connection. Analogical reasoning would seem to be involved in citing illegibility as an indication of dissimulation, and the production of small writing as an evidence of love of minutiae. A similar kind of induction is apparently involved in the relation assumed between an extensive movement of the penpoint above the line-heavenward as it were!—and idealistic proclivities, and ascription of earthly or materialistic qualities to the penman producing long down-strokes.

Note: Mental Adjustments, p. 93.

2. *Appeal to Psychological Principles.*

The literature of graphology makes frequent appeal to psychological principles. I have accordingly been somewhat surprised to find that my reading has precipitated so little in the way of definite reference of graphological interpretations to the specific psychology of movement. A few citations are made to bear the weight of an elaborate superstructure.

a. The general tendency of every psychic state to issue in some form of movement is frequently cited as fundamental to the graphological position although a limitation to its serviceability as a principle of interpretation may be recognized not only in its extreme generality but also in the difficulty in application due to individual differences in the expressive threshold.

b. A second law appealed to is that of dynamogeny, namely, that the force and energy of movement are a direct outcome of mental energy, which is, in turn, conditioned to a degree by external factors such as external illumination, temperature, writing apparatus, etc. Size of writing and pressure are two graphic elements interpretation of which is referred to this general principle. The magnified writing of the ambitious and the minute penmanship of the tired or cautious person are described as well as the heavy stroke of the strong-willed and the light stroke of the weak-willed penman.

c. A third principle is the so-called law of emotional expression which correlates centrifugal and centripetal movement with joyful and depressed moods respectively. The treatment is assimilated to much that we are familiar with in other applications of emotional expression, for instance, the Delsartean system of eccentric and concentric postures.

Granting that the general assumption of emotional expression is well grounded, we find some very dubious applications of it in graphology. Mainly such application is to be found in dealing with the significance of slant and alignment. Thus falling alignment is a symptom of depression like the dragging footstep; rising alignment is indicative of hopefulness. Back-slant is symptomatic of reserve just as extreme right slant betokens emotional susceptibility and vertical writing indicates emotional control.

Two other principles of interpretation are cited by Klages. (**26a**). One (d) he calls the law of periodic fluctuation of attention which results in relaxation of control at certain parts of lines, words, and letters and hence makes it possible to discriminate between voluntary and spontaneous graphic traits. Klages' chief contribution, however, concerns (e) the operation of impulsion and inhibition in determining certain graphic patterns. The application of such a psychological principle does not favor the mechanical listing of isolated graphic traits with their respective significance so much as it does the discovery of the possible combination of specific symptoms and their common reference to the general motor organization of the individual.

Klages also cites in explanation of certain graphic signs a law of so-called feeling for spatial analogy; the implication being, I take it, that in certain cases a delicate application of Empathy operates in determining preference for certain forms and slants.

3. *Empirical Observation and Comparative Study.*

The empirical method consists in extensive study and comparison of handwritings. Thus the hands of persons of known common traits are compared and a conclusion drawn as to the way in which a given psychic character manifests itself in script. Or a certain grouping of hands results from one's study and may lead to a cataloguing of the mental traits possessed by the penman in order to determine whether there are any that are common to the group. Scholarly graphologists amass collections of writing specimens which may be utilized in the twofold way mentioned above. Thus they may institute comparison between the hand-writing specimens found in collections coming from the intellectually inferior and the intellectually superior and seek the graphic symptoms of intellectual superiority or inferiority. They may compare the chirography of criminals with that of moral reformers and so on. This method may be refined to any degree, with an application of the classic method of agreement and difference.

In any case a criticism urged by Mr. Osborn is undoubtedly valid, namely, that too little information is current among graphologists as to the general effect upon script of the writing system learned. These systems vary not only from one nation to another but within a given country from one decade to another. Thus in the United States alone it is possible to trace the vogue of at least five systems; namely, the old English round hand; the modified round hand; the Spencerian system; the modern vertical; and, in addition, an angular style taught in schools for girls. Difference in designs of letters, difference in proportions between letter-parts, difference in slant and shading will characterize the script of those taught different systems. Moreover, mannerisms from foreign systems may cling to a style; thus the influence of German script on writing is a very perceptible one. The unsophisticated observer may find striking similarities and differences in two writings that have no significance whatever other than witnessing similarity or difference in the system of writing that was learned originally. As an outcome of this masking of the individual chirography by national and epochal habits it would seem that we must seek for the distinctive graphic sign of say diplomacy or candor or imagination in penmen who have learned different systems of writing or we may institute a comparison of hands for determination of a particular difference only when confident that in general the penmen have learned the same system of writing.

But there are other factors which might influence the grouping of a collection of samples but which have only a limited psychodiagnostic significance. The best graphologists are perfectly well aware of these contributing elements and have given us a more or less detailed treatment of them. W may list these factors as follows: education and amount of practice in handwriting; professional requirements which determine the vertical hand of the librarian, or the print-like hand of the engineer; age; sex; fatigue; and disease. A word as to the significance of each.

A number of observations point to a fairly general recognition of certain differences between the writing of the educated and the uncultivated. The chirography of the latter shows an unaccustomedness, an awkwardness, an inexpertness that marks it rather unmistakeably. But one cannot always apply the contrasting adjectives to the hand of the educated except in so far as accustomedness is concerned. It too may be both awkward and without grace, although usually rapid. The fundamental difference grows out of amount of practice in using the pen. Practice is evident in the greater speed and smoothness with which the graphic product is produced. There exists, however, a so-called cultured hand which indicates breeding to a very high degree. It possesses both grace and distinction as well as the facility that is the result of much use of the pen. With the increasing utilization of the typist such hands are becoming rarer and the educated man is satisfied with a scrawl as a mark of identification.

Since practice is so great a factor in development of graphic virtuosity, we are not surprised to find certain lines of work leaving an imprint upon chirography. The teacher's hand is conventional. The clerical hand is marked by ease of manner, speed and greater or less conventionality. Even more conventional, very deliberate and slow is the vertical hand of the cataloguer. The telegrapher's hand is rapid, fluent, marked by a definite style and exhibiting certain mannerisms as to the number of words per line and the like. Such hands are often cited in support of the position that handwriting individuality is the product of objective factors only. Graphic virtuosity, with its accompanying speed and satisfactoriness of outcome, is the result of correct and prolonged practice. All of us might, it is assumed, acquire the rapid business hand or the artistic print of the mechanic. The assumption is a big one. As have been urged before, hands that show to a very high degree the possibility of voluntary control undoubtedly exist, but not every one can produce them. Not every one can acquire as a permanent possession the smooth, rapid, highly legible clerical or business hand. A process of selection goes on so that the individual who finds himself limited on the side of graphic facility drops out of the race early. As the reverse to this picture we may point out the existence of families of clerks, one of whose assets is a rapid legible hand, pleasing in appearance. I could cite many instances in the community with which I am best acquainted where the easy acquisition of a ready handwriting has been noted for many members of the same family, and for two or three generations. In one case this graphic ease has determined the line of work adopted by many of the group.

Age is also a very definite factor conditioning handwriting. In part, of course, it is a question again of amount of practice. With increasing age comes increased motor skill. In part, it is a question of varying degree of dominance of a hand by the conventional standards of the system learned. The young hand is less individual. In the decline that comes with old age indicative signs appear in the writing. Loss of motor control may be manifested by tremor; often writing is increased in size, because of failing eye-sight or as a compensation for ataxia; there is an approximation to the so-called masculine type.

Very real as these symptoms are, the deduction of age of penman from a given handwriting is by no means easy. Binet in his test of professional graphologists found that age could be determined with some degree of accuracy, on the average within about ten years (**3c**) but that there were many specimens that gave little indication of age or even gave a false indication. I have already spoken of the curious difference in the time at which writing sets, as a family characteristic. In the case of a late maturing or setting of handwriting we may get the impression of immature or child-like hands from specimens produced by well-developed individuals. I have long been curious as to the explanation for this late setting of handwriting. Instances that have particularly attracted my attention include three cases of very brilliant young men, gifted in law or literature, whose intellectual development has been remarkably precocious but whose hands have "ripened" very slowly. I am inclined to think that a late maturing of a hand is an indication of a "sensory" make-up; an early maturing of a "motor" make-up, a distinction to which we shall return later.

Sex as a determinant of handwriting has been dealt with at some length by investigators. Mostly, graphologists are somewhat conservative concerning the possibility of deducing sex from handwriting. Binet's test of graphologists showed that their successes in detecting sex from handwriting ranged from 63 to 78.8 per cent, and under favorable conditions might reach 90 per cent (**3c**), figures which were confirmed by a later experiment by myself. (**14c**). Curious inversion of sex-signs were, however, discovered by experimentation so that many women are found to write hands that are unanimously chosen as masculine hands and a few men write unmistakeably ladylike hands. The interpretation of the situation is somewhat ambiguous, since sex in writing may be largely an outcome of social factors which emphasize neatness, grace, conventionality in the woman's hand and speed, force, and originality in the man's. On the other hand, Meumann (**32**) reports a masculine and a feminine type of hand, differentiated by the appearance of characteristic pressure curves, types which if confirmed would evidence rather fundamental differences in kind of motor control.

The effect of fatigue and of disease upon writing opens up an extensive field for exploration. Professor Janet, of the College de France, urges that experimental graphology should begin with studies in pathological graphology, studies on the effect upon handwriting of diseases of motility and sensibility, or of specific diseases, such as those of respiration and of circulation. From the more pronounced modifications of handwriting transitions may then be made to its more delicate inflections. This recourse to pathology bids fair to prove increasingly fruitful and deserves treatment in a separate section.

Within these generic types as outlined above, the graphologist must conduct his search for character-complexes, guarding always not only against confusion of the generic with the individual but also against the accidental variations that are due to purely objective factors such as writing apparatus, illumination, haste, social requirements, etc. It is the complexity of the problem that leads many psychologists to question the possibility of a serviceable psychodiagnosis from handwriting. They may grant the revelatory character of movement and yet despair of any very specific utilization of it so far as writing is concerned. Yet precipitates from the extensive study and comparison of handwriting specimens by able observers certainly deserve consideration. If nothing else, their conclusions afford suggestions for an experimental program.

If I may judge from my own experience, observation of handwriting results in what may be described as conceptual precipitates, composite images, very similar to the generic images of facial types. I find myself mentally classifying hands as belonging to the "smooth flowing" type or the "labored inhibited" type or the "rapid, explosive" type. Such categories have developed from my experience quite without deliberation, although I find that I possess fairly clear-cut visual images of one or two specific hands that may stand as representative of a particular type. My mental fixation of a hand involves its classification with a particular group. My failure to note details is surprising but in spite of it or perhaps because of it I have a rather unusual capacity for recognition and memory of hands. My composite images of hands have developed in connection with study of individuals so that as part of my classification I am apt to question myself as to whether the penman in question belongs temperamentally with the group in which his writing places him. Thus the "flowing" type of hand has so often in my experience been produced by the socially tactful, adjustable, often charming, sometimes merely plausible, individual that I find it creates a definite expectation.

In addition to these "generic images" of hands that have resulted in part, from a native interest in graphic expression, and, in part, from extensive preoccupation with chirography as a material for experimental work, I find a second factor involved in my sensing a personality from handwriting. This second factor may be described as an attempt, although not an overt one, at motor mimicry or imitative interpretation. I find myself imaging kinesthetically the type of movement suggested by a given handwriting. The imitation results in a feeling of the assumption of a foreign personality. The general method is similar to an attempt to get a clue concerning the permanent temper or casual mood of another by mimicry of his walk or his attitude. Whoever has tried copying another's carriage, his manner, for example, of carrying his crooked arms with elbows outspread in true Irish fashion or hugging the body in diffidence is aware how enlightening such mimicry may be. The suppressed mimicry of a graphic pattern is, of course, a much more subtle matter. In my own case it is released only by very individual hands and only when I am in certain frames of mind. I have, however, seen such a method utilized in very explicit form by a little girl of ten years who once served me as subject. This child had recourse in the most naive way to mimicry by facial expression and bodily contortion of the handwriting she was observing.

4. *The Method of Intuition.*

In the section on the concept of the graphological portrait we saw that there is a point at which graphologists abandon an analytical for a synthetic method of procedure. In dealing with handwriting as material for study I am, therefore, tempted to discuss a little more fully the opposition between a deliberate and an intuitional handling of material. This discussion is motivated by two observations, first, the extraordinary differences that normal individuals show in their capacity to recognize and remember handwritings; and, secondly, by the distrust of the handwriting expert of judgments based on general appearance of writing.

Binet in his investigation of the extent to which age, sex, intelligence, and morality could be told from script found that such measure of success as was achieved by professionals could be approximated by amateurs. My experience with reagents in an experiment on the sex judgment resulted similarly. (**14c**). R, in particular—a highly sensitive young woman with decided literary and artistic gifts—gave evidence of extraordinary facility. Her record is very nearly as accurate as that of Crépieux-Jamin, the French expert. R. reported a very definite sensing of personality from writing, the accuracy of which could not be tested as her help was available only for the one series of experiments.

In a number of other experiments in which handwriting has been used as material a great individual variation in facility in handling it is evident, quite apart from training or extensive experience with it. In an experiment in which reagents matched pairs of addresses written by a given number of penmen, I found not only a wide range of variation in ability but also an approximation of the best record by a girl of eleven years. In an experiment on disguised handwriting I found one wholly unpracticed reagent whose penetration of a disguise excelled that of very careful students of the subject. Osborn found a practical application for such individual difference in its negative aspect; failure to see similarity in handwriting often makes it impossible for a judge to follow the line of argument presented by a handwriting expert in court. The Osborn test for determination of what he calls form-blindness—namely the search for samples of words written by the same penmen—revealed a wide range of variation in individual records, namely, from 100 per cent accuracy in 8 minutes and 35 seconds to 65 per cent of accuracy in 9 minutes and 55 seconds." (**36:6**) Bingham (**4**) reports, in comparison with other tests, a very high coefficient of variability for the Osborn test.

That the amateur should so closely approximate the record of the professional points to an interesting problem, if only the identification of a field of work in which practice effects are at a minimum. It raises the question, for a specific situation, of the value of the intuitional method. Dearborn (**11b**) has recently analyzed in most profitable fashion what he conceives to be involved in intuition and he has urged the psychologist to enter upon a scientific investigation of this very promising concept. Rather than approach the problem as a variation in sex-intelligence, as Dearborn suggests, it would seem more auspicious to map out the field on the basis of different materials. Specialized virtuosity in any field and, in particular, the automatic processes of art would suggest themselves as promising material for analysis. The contributions of both original capacity and extensive training could possibly be laid bare.

In my experience with reagents in tests on handwriting I have noted two varying tendencies; one a preoccupation with graphic details, the other a preoccupation with the general appearance of the hand in question. I cannot say on the basis of the results which is generally the more successful; but there can be no question that in some instances a preoccupation with details has completely blinded a reagent to very striking individuality. It is with considerable astonishment that I have observed the insensitiveness to general appearance of certain very careful and highly intelligent reagents who compare varying details with most painful exactness and yet totally miss the graphic pattern. This point I have discussed elsewhere (**14,d**) but only in such a way as to set the problem. Possibly we have here an instance of judgment of general likeness (impressionistic) versus one based on specific difference.

The problem involved is very extensive in its application. Work in systematic botany and zoology reveals, I am told, the same sort of distinction in scientists. A too-great preoccupation with similarities may lead to an oversight of differences that may prove basal from a classificatory standpoint, while preoccupation with differences may result in the endless splitting of subdivisions. In an experiment on handwriting similarity and difference I sought to determine whether there existed an individual difference in the readiness with which difference or similarity was perceived. The results seemed to indicate that most reagents are able to shift somewhat easily from one mental set to another but that there were reagents who were actually more successful in maintaining one or the other of the two sets. The most striking example of facility with likeness and incapacity to handle differences occurred in the case of a girl whose failure in botanical classifications was in great contrast to her usual academic success.

The handwriting expert in court procedure is most distrustful of a judgment based on general appearance of handwriting. In study of handwriting he recommends placing word by word and letter by letter the material from the disputed document and the possible original. His judgment is the outcome of the most refined measurement and comparison of details. There can be no question of the justness of the expert's insistance upon the methodical and exacting testing of a questioned document nor his scepticism of the unchecked and biased testimony of the average undiscriminating witness. But it would, none the less, be of great value to institute a comparison under controlled conditions of the judgment of a picked reagent based on general appearance and that of the expert based on a comparison of details. The latter method makes possible a simpler process of presentation of proof, although enlarged photographs might serve in the former case.

5. *Experimental Graphology.*

Graphological exploration has not been conducted solely by empirical or intuitive methods. Actual experimentation has been resorted to, although it has only been by slow degrees that a critical understanding has been evolved as to the precise problems under consideration and the control of conditions necessary for satisfactory work. But a gradual refinement of method of experimentation with increasing understanding of the points at issue is, of course, inherent in the development of every investigation.

Basal to every attempt at experiment has been the idea of concomitant variation, change in writing with change in conditions under which it has been produced. Thus the concept of graphic variability is found to be essential to the general hypothesis of grapho-psychodiagnosis and not a mere embarrassment as many critics have assumed.

The earliest experiments, as resumed by Crépieux-Jamin, impress us as extremely ambitious in intention and vague in execution. **(9:127f)**. Yet since the question at issue is that of the revelation of a personality through writing it is not surprising that early attempts at testing this assumption in the experiments conducted by Ferrari, Hericourt, and Richet consisted in seeking to determine the effect upon handwriting of suggesting successive personalities to hynotized subjects. They conclude that "the written gesture is transformed as is the gesture in general" **(9:128)** and that, in consequence, it is proved that variations in writing are a function of variations in personality. The vagueness of the conception of personality renders such experiments of little significance. In a later attempt to render experimentation more definite comes the device of suggesting to the hypnotised subject that he assume the personality of a historic character of very definite individuality. The writing produced under such suggestion may then be compared with that proceeding from the character thus simulated!

Crépieux-Jamin recognizing the limitations of the hypnotic method, in so far as the subject never completely loses his personality, rejected the method as unnecessarily complicated and used simple persuasion. The reagent, unacquainted with graphology, is first asked to write a given phrase in his natural way, and then, under definite emotional suggestion, is asked to write it again. The method is said to be usable only when the subject is both susceptible to suggestion and intelligent.

It is scarcely necessary to enter upon criticism of the attempt to alter the fundamental individuality of a hand. In addition to difficulties in the way of manipulating the reagent, the subjective element in interpretation of results would be overwhelming. But where deep-seated changes in personality actually occur, as in alternating personalities, a detailed comparison between the handwriting in the two states should prove most illuminating if there be anything at all in the graphological contention. But the material at hand is very meagre. Dr. Prince records instances of "Sally's inability to write when badly 'squeezed.' She was then obliged to resort to printing; sometimes both printed and written characters were illegible. Ordinarily her handwriting is like that of the primary personalities—" (40:56lf)

De Fursac, commenting on the modifications from the normal in the case of mediumistic writing, reports that they are more apparent than real. They result often in writing being larger or smaller than the normal writing or in the slant being modified. But the modifications are for the most part said to be superficial so that it is not difficult to recognize the fundamental characters of the normal writing of the medium. Unfortunately, however, we possess only a few reproductions of mediumistic writing submitted with copies of the normal chirography. An extensive collection might prove of great interest.

Experimental graphology must, however, content itself with a more modest procedure than an attempt to solve all problems by one device. It has, as a matter of fact, made slow but real progress by attacking three topics which may be listed as follows: (a) The limits of objective conditions as determinants of individuality and the specific variations for which each is responsible; (b) The range and explanation for variation in the writing of a given individual—apart, of course, from variation due to objective conditions—and the range of variation from one individual to another; (c) The range of voluntary control, with specific determination of the graphic elements that may be easily modified and of those that resist modification.

(a) It is not difficult to list objective factors which might affect handwriting but it is very difficult to determine the range of effect. Some of these factors have already been mentioned. They include such conditions as quality of ink, quality and size and position of writing surface, fineness or coarseness of pen, objective illumination and temperature, external pressure in the maintenance of speed or legibility, form of movement employed,—finger, wrist, or forearm. Our estimate of the actual effect of such factors on writing is, to be sure, somewhat crude. Other factors more intimately associated with the penman's make-up would include influence of unconscious imitation (**43**), effect of written content, effect of bodily fatigue and of specific drugs such as alcohol. (**30**) Crépieux-Jamin has reported variations in his writing under changes in weather, fatigue, illumination, visual supervision and the like. (**9:136f**) He has also cited changes produced by various emotional conditions.

(b) This last marks a transition to the second topic, namely specific variation under specific changes in subjective conditions, variation in mood, emotional excitement, sensory control and varying degree of impulsion. In such an investigation, if anywhere, graphologists must find a justification for assigning specific significance to specific graphic traits. But variation is two sorts; variation from one individual to another and variation in the written products of the same individual; there is inter-individual and intra-individual variation. Can one conclude because the writing of a given individual varies in a characteristic fashion under given conditions that one is justified in a similar interpretation of variations in different hands?

The question is a vital one. To give a definite example. There can be no question that the handwriting of a given individual varies in size with change in sensory control. With increased attention to writing we get a decrease in size, except under certain conditions which need not be specified here, while with distraction of attention from writing we get magnification of script. This outcome of experimentation enables us to explain some interesting variations in size of writing for a given individual but what bearing has it upon variation in size of hand from one individual to another? The parallelism is not as simple a one as appears upon the face of it. Is one justified in concluding that a hand relatively small is a sign of preoccupation with writing as a process and that large writing is due to automatism of control? The question can be answered only by an extensive comparison of the handwriting of reagents of known mental habits. But in any case how set up a group standard for size, particularly in view of the fact of individual variation in the expressive threshold?

If one may parallel group and individual variation, it would seem that the interpretation of the significance of size, pressure, slant and alignment should be determined by study of their variation in the individual and that the significance of proportion and continuity should be determined by inter-individual comparison.

(c) The question of the range of voluntary control for writing as a whole and for each graphic sign has been tested in the experiments on disguised and retarded handwriting. A summary of these experiments will appear in the experimental section. Suffice it to say here that, according to Meyer, such experiments enable us to determine which elements are produced under supervision of attention, which are spontaneous products of motor-impulses. Thus slant, size, and form are found to be more artificially produced than proportion, degree of continuity and alignment. Moreover, by noting the specific effect of increased attention upon writing—which is a result of an attempt at disguise—we are enabled to determine just what traits characterize the controlled hand in contrast with the spontaneous one. Size and slant, for example, are decreased in the disguised hand, and there are more breaks in continuity with an emphasis of the long down-stroke, results which lead us to attribute to such a hand when it occurs under normal conditions a higher degree of self-control (inhibition) than we attribute to larger, more inclined, more continuous script.

One word more, it is not easy to say where graphological experimentation—testing the hypothesis that writing may be used in psychodiagnosis—ends and psychological experimentation begins. Certainly the psychology of handwriting as such should be utilized by a scientific graphology, while grapho-psychodiagnosis if ever substantiated would become a part of applied psychology. We shall find in our more specific discussions considerable overlapping of fields of work. One very great difference in point of view should, however, be pointed out. The psychology of handwriting is concerned mainly with a study of the writing movement; graphology is concerned with the written product. The former method is highly analytic and has worked out accurate methods for observation as detailed in the Kraepelinian studies where precise instruments for registration of pressure and speed and size are described (**13:22:30**). Freeman's fine investigation of the writing movement also necessitates a command of instrumental technique. (**16ac**). Psychologists interested in such detailed analyses are apt to dismiss the graphological program as premature in its interest even if not absurdly ambitious in design. Eventually, perhaps, the psychology of handwriting may have something to offer in the way of psychodiagnosis. Meanwhile there is much elementary work to be done.

For practical purposes, however, judgment must be passed on the graphic product, not the graphic process. This has been evidenced by the evolution of handwriting scales as a pedagogical device. (**2:46a**). Nor can the utilization of writing in psychodiagnosis proceed far unless transition is possible from the movement to the product of movement. Freeman, however, is reported as directing a handwriting investigation by means of the kinetoscope which suggests far-reaching possibilities, one of which may be a convenient method of studying many individual hands in the process of making. (Note.)

NOTE—See Journal Applied Psychology 1, 1917, p. 298.

6. *Pathological Writing.*

Graphologists and others interested in handwriting have long realized that in pathological writing they have a fertile field for work. We have already seen how Janet urged that investigation of the significance of graphic symptoms should begin with determination of the changes in writing that take place under definite pathological conditions. Graphologists have also realized the value of such material and usually include in their discussions some reference to pathological writing.

Pathologists, approaching the subject from a totally different standpoint, have sought to utilize writing in differential diagnosis of disease. They have had little interest in psychodiagnosis as such; they have, rather, been searching for signs of specific disturbances in the writing of patients. Such a collection as the most interesting one by Dr. Kőster had this for its object. He gives characteristic hands for patients suffering from chorea, hysteria, senile paralysis, dementia precox, etc. (**27**) Clinicians who present specimens of this sort in connection with case histories often fail to make any distinction between utilization of graphic elements as such and utilization of the written content. Often, of course, disturbances of attention, of memory, and of speech-function are evident in the written content quite apart from any specific grapho-motor disturbance. Pen-lapses are usually analyzed as a product of mental disorders and not scrutinized for evidence of concurrent disturbance of motility.

Not only do workers in this field fail at times to discriminate between graphic and contentual disturbances but, in general, they fail to realize the necessity of presenting the normal writing of a patient for comparison with the pathological. For adequate comparison one should have a series of samples showing the progressive effect of the disease upon the writing. So inadequate, however, has been the conception of the requirements for satisfactory comparison that much of the material that has been published is of very little value.

The same situation is evident in study of pathological drawings. Năcke (**35b**) has drawn attention to the need of samples of normal drawings by the patient for comparison with pathological productions. He makes the particular point that inexpertness or lack of training may give a drawing an appearance of being pathological or atavistic in intent although it might be duplicated easily by drawings from the mentally normal. Năcke's strictures are worth heeding. None the less, there seems a residue from the work on pathological drawing that indicates the possibility of utilizing in some degree drawing in diagnosis. The stereotyped productions of the catatonics, and the symbolistic pictures of the dementia precox patient probably have symptomatic value.

The application of conclusions derived from study of pathological writing to psychodiagnosis in general is not a simple one, and certainly not to be settled by a priori considerations. Whether or not pathological writing exhibits psychomotor correspondences writ beg is a question to be answered only after elaborate study.

De Fursac, without attempting to pass judgment upon the outcome of graphological observation, remarks that in any case the correspondences reported for normal cases do not hold simply under pathological conditions and he presents his material in such a way as to make comparison with the traditional treatment of the graphic signs easy to achieve. (**18**).

Hirt (**23a**) makes a threefold distinction of obvious importance but one that is frequently ignored. Quite apart from physical conditions the writing-act can proceed adequately only if the integrity of the motor apparatus be preserved. Hence it is necessary (a) to study the physiological conditions of writing and to note those cases of pathological writing that indicate structural changes, gross anatomical changes possibly; (b) to work out in detail the psychophysics of writing, the correlation of determined mental conditions with peculiarities of action; and (c) to consider characteristics of pathological writing that are more specifically psychological, independent, that is, of physiological conditions.

From the physiological side the investigation of writing demands consideration of the general conditions of voluntary movement and of motor coordination, including the part played in coordination by visual sensations and sensations from the moving parts. Clinical experience shows that insensitive limbs may be brought under eye-control. Skill once acquired is lost only under certain conditions, as in ataxia. The writing of the ataxic, both with eyes open and eyes closed, merits careful study. The psychophysics of writing involves study of individual variations in both reflex and voluntary movements. Through observations of the tendency to and *intensity* of movements which a man employs in order to gain a certain end, important conclusions may be drawn relative to his personality. Individual types of behavior are to be sought in the *temporal* relations of movement; in the writing reaction-types, where the author claims to have found experimentally a *sensorial* and a *motor* course; in *pressure-types,* corresponding to the *sensory* and *motor* reaction-types; in *rhythmic peculiarities;* and in *variations* in *rapidity* of writing and in *fluctuations* in rapidity. Numerous problems are raised, as, for example, the cause of the increase or decrease of writing-size when writing is produced with the eyes closed.

In dealing with mental diseases that are characterized largely by mental symptoms, Hirt appears to find a point of departure for the characterological study of handwriting. "How discriminate with security," he asks, "the writing of a maniac or melancholic from that of a motorly excited or motorly inhibited man?" In the majority of cases, pathological writing is differentiated from handwriting marked by personal peculiarities only by the heightening of such peculiarities. Such comparison of the handwriting of temperamental and insane subjects raises a question which psychiatrists are still debating, the existence, that is, of certain make-ups which are basal both to character varieties and anomalies, and to specific forms of insanity which may result in case of strain. (**33:42**).

In any case it is urged by competent authority, in agreement with the experimental psychologists, that the study of pathological writing should not be based on observation of the graphic product but that there should be regression to analytic registration of the graphic movements of the patients who are under investigation. It is thought that such utilization of writing-movements may have actual diagnostic significance.

CHAPTER IV.

THE GRAPHOLOGICAL ELEMENTS.

In order to confine our discussion to certain definite issues let us now consider a few interpretations that have resulted as a precipitate from graphological analysis. And in order to give these interpretations background let us attempt a comparative survey by means of which we may bring into relationship the different possible methods of approach. Our procedure will be as follows. Out of the myriad intricacies, the subtle distinctions, given us in the treatises on the subject we will choose a few graphic elements and subject them to definite scrutiny from the following points of view: (1) the graphological; (2) the pathological (following de Fursac); (3) that of the handwriting expert (following Osborn); and (4) that of experimental investigation whether motivated by graphological or psychological interest. We will carry our schematism so far as to attempt a tabular summary of this comparative survey.

The graphic elements chosen for such exploitation are the following: (I) Size, or dimension; (II) Pressure and line-quality; (III) Direction, including slant and alignment; (IV) Continuity; (V) Proportion. Some violence is done the graphological position by an undue simplification of it but a certain amount of simplification is necessary in the interest of a clear-cut presentation.

I. *Graphic Dimension.*

1. In this presentation we will limit ourselves largely to discussion of letter-size. The graphologists tell us that a "big" hand is a sign of imagination, or ambition, or pride. The particular form that ambition or pride may assume will be determined by the general setting in which size is only one element. Minute writing is a symptom of preoccupation with minutiae; of finesse; of miserliness or, sometimes, myopia. Again, the general setting is important. Varia-

tions in size are also significant; diminution in size as writing proceeds indicates ambition or ardor that plays out; increase indicates waxing ardor.

The determination of whether letters shall be considered large or small offers considerable difficulty. "Miniscules" less than two millimeters in height may, however, be cited as small; and capitals that are less than eight millimeters. Small letters that run above three millimeters are big and capitals that are more than twelve millimeters high. (Note) Often, graphologists appear to utilize the capitals alone as sufficiently indicative of character traits. In this connection they also make much of the variations in form of the capital and the possibility it offers for excess decoration.

The characterological interpretation appears to be based on feeling for size as contributing to prestige; the more "consequential" a conscious state is felt to be, the more impetus toward "large" expression.

2. Let us turn now to pathological writing. Is increase or decrease of graphic dimensions indicative of any particular mental condition? De Fursac writes (**18:13f**): The dimension of letters is in large measure a function of the psychomotor activity or energy. Psychomotor exaltation or hyperkinesis manifests itself under two different forms which may be combined in variable proportions, increase in rapidity of the graphic movements and increase in the extension and energy of these movements. Specifically, so far as extent of movement is concerned, we find that augmentation of extent of movement leads to an increase in the height of letters. The extent of such magnification is clearly evident when the normal writing of a patient is compared with that produced in a state of maniacal excitement. Increased rapidity of writing as shown by timed records is also an outcome of such excitement. The relation of such increased speed to amplitude is of great interest. When increase in rapidity does not exceed certain limits it remains

Note—Cf. Graves, S. M. "A Study of Handwriting," Journal of Educational Psychology, p. 483-494.

compatible with increase in the height of letters, and amplitude and speed are associated. But when speed becomes very great the inverse phenomenon occurs, namely, a diminution in size of letters, a diminution which may result in certain words being reduced to vague undulating lines, quite illegible. Often in the same specimen we find both manifestations of hyperkinesis,—increase in height and diminution of movement due to excessive speed.

The enfeeblement of psychomotor activity manifests itself, in general, in a diminution in the height of letters, conjoined not with increased rapidity but with retardation of the graphic movement. Specimens are given of such decrease in size under conditions of melancholy depression. (**18:15**)

Sometimes a sample of writing from the same patient shows great variability in size. Fatigue, for example, may lead to writing that becomes progressively more diminished in amplitude, while under the influence of automatism writing increases in size, a fact strikingly evident in stereotypy. Extreme variability in size may be the outcome of variation in speed or it may be determined by diminution in the power of attention. (**18:19**)

Specific mental disorders furnish examples of such shifts in size. Thus the writing of the dementia precox patient may be normal in size or very large or very extenuated depending upon the dominance of automatism or hyperkinesis or fatigue. (**18:151**). Even the manic does not always produce greatly magnified writing; sometimes irregularity in size is more characteristic than is increase in dimensions. (**18:198**). Very great decrease in size from the normal may occur in the case of melancholic depression, such decrease being greater in spontaneous writing than in writing under dictation, because of the greater mental effort involved in the former case. But, as before, irregularity in size testifies to the disturbance of attention. (**18:211f.**)

Other specialists on pathological writing are in pretty fair agreement with de Fursac. Both Kőster (**27**) and Hirt (**23a:399**) reproduce specimens showing magnified writing when the patient is in his manic period and very minute writing produced under conditions of depression. Decrease in size through fatigue is substantiated. Kőster reports, also, an increase in size of writing resorted to in an unconscious attempt to mask lack of motor control—a device that I have noted in elderly people.

Gross (**22:498**), following the more exact technique of the Kraepelinian investigations, found retardation of speed, reduction in size, and sub-normal pressure during depression in circular insanity. Writing characters became progressively smaller instead of showing the more normal increase in size. In mania, Gross reports that results were less clear-cut. With rising excitement there was, however, a tendency to increased speed, increased size and increased pressure.

Hirt (**23a:397f**) reports: The melancholic patient enters upon the writing act with great slowness and with anxiety. The stroke of single lines is at times surprisingly weak and the letters not seldom exceedingly minute. The maniac, on the contrary, seizes the pen boldly and dashes off the given proposition in large energetic strokes. On the mental side the melancholic gives a picture of inhibition, pedantry, anxiety, poverty of thought, self-depreciation; the maniac exhibits want of consideration, thoughtlessness, incoherence, self-exaltation.

3. Letter-size, the expert informs us, is largely dependent upon the writing system which has been learned. Variations in this respect are not significant in identification of writing unless they are extreme. Many external factors influence letter-size. Thus the fineness or coarseness of the pen with which one is writing will influence the size of graphic product. Often, too, the amplitude of the sheet upon which one writes is a significant factor. Everyone produces a microscopic hand in addressing a doll's envelope, and a large one in labelling an express package. It is fairly easy to alter size voluntarily and within wide limits.

Spacing, Osborn tells us (**36a:149**) "is mainly changed by the slant of the upward or connecting stroke," a habit which is also dependent upon the system of writing which one has learned. The old round hand and the modern vertical show greater compactness than a Spencerian hand.

4. Size, together with speed and pressure, is a graphic element that has been subjected to considerable experimental observation. The Kraepelin studies (**13:22**) have given particular attention to it and Freeman (**16c**) has contributed a detailed analysis.

There are some interesting relationships observable between size and speed. A graphic rhythm develops in which there is an attempt to keep the time element constant for a given form even under changed conditions of size. In general, we find increased size correlated with increased speed; there is also progressive increase in size as writing continues, closely related again to developing speed. As attention is withdrawn from writing there is an increase in size, particularly evident in automatic writing. Writing that is produced with the eyes closed also shows, normally, an increase in size, although there are many exceptions to this statement.

Decrease in size of graphic movement is an outcome of lessened speed or of INTENTIONAL increase in speed. It occurs, in general, whenever effort is involved in handling the situation. The direction of attention to the writing movement as in disguised writing leads to a decrease in size, although this tendency may be overcome by voluntary increase of dimensions and in exceptional cases the slow writing approaches the conventional standard and therefore becomes larger.

Cutting through these results we find, moreover, small writing as an outcome of graphic expertness. Illiterate writing is large because of lack of motor control.

All of the above statements, it should be observed, refer directly to changes in the extent of graphic movement when we are dealing with a particular individual under given experimental conditions. To what degree we are justified in attempting to apply any of these experimental findings in an inter-individual comparison of hands is very doubtful. An extremely large and free hand may, however, indicate general freedom of impulse while an abnormally small hand would lead to suspicion of the presence of inhibitory tendencies which might vary considerably in nature. Small writing may be due to excess of control or to economy of effort as an outcome of practice and skill; it may indicate self-consciousness and inhibition or it may evidence expertness.

Dearborn (**11,a**) in a series of experiments in which a figure was learned by motor tracery found that concentration on the conscious movement-sensations led to decreased extent of movement. He concludes that the conscious movement sensations are inhibitory in function. There are, he thinks, two phases of kinesthesia, one unconscious and actuating, the other conscious and inhibitory in function. From this it may follow that large writing is, in general, produced by the less controlled, more automatic penmen, while small writing is indicative of concentration on the writing movement or, perhaps, on the external product.

Interpretation of Size of Letters

GRAPHOLOGICAL	MECHANICAL	PATHOLOGICAL	EXPERIMENTAL
Absolutely large writing: pride, ambition, imagination. Spaced writing: clearness generosity. Small or filiform script; love of detail, critical acumen, pedantry, finesse. Compressed writing: parsimony, self-centeredness. Minute writing may be due to myopia.	Size of letters depends largely on system of writing and on musculature utilized. It is greatly influenced by external factors, such as pen, size of paper, etc. "The spacing of writing is mainly changed by the slant of the upward or connecting stroke." (Osborn.)	Psycho-motor excitement shown in increased extent of writing, as in manias, exaltation. Automatism leads to increase in dimensions. Loss of motor control may be masked by magnification of script. Psycho-motor enfeeblement results in reduced writing. Small writing characterizes melancholia. Fatigue may lead to a decrease in size of script.	Increased size accompanies increased nervous activity (Anregung). Initial impulse increases size at beginning of writing (Antrieb). Automatic writing produced with distraction of attention shows increase in dimensions. Script produced with the eyes closed is usually larger than normal. Decrease in size is associated with lessened speed. But, also, decrease in size comes with increase in graphic expertness. Decrease in dimensions of graphic characters occurs when effort is involved or when attention is directed to writing movement. Decrease in size is an outcome of *intentional* increase in speed. Self-conscious writing is frequently small and a disguised hand is often reduced in size from the normal.

2. *Force of Movement; Pressure, Line-Quality.*

1. The particular graphic quality with which we are dealing in this section is somewhat difficult to define. The reference is to intensity or strength of movement as indicated by heaviness or delicacy of the line-quality, its smoothness and regularity. Involuntary placing of emphasis, as distinguished from conventional shading, is in question. The general graphological assumption appears to be that strong firm heavy lines are the outcome of actual pressure against the surface of the paper and that this, in turn, is an expression of strong will-impulse. Force of will is deduced from emphatic and firm movements; weakness of will from delicate and tremulous line-stroke. Transitional forms occur; persistence is shown by regularity of pressure; spurts of energy and force by abrupt pressure. The club and staccato strokes as they appear in the crossing of the "t" or in punctuation marks are thought to be significant.

The explanation for such interpretation is cited as self-evident; namely, that strength and energy of will express themselves in forceful and energetic movement. It is, however, observed that heavy wide lines in contrast to fine tracery are not always the outcome of resolute movement. The writing materials, such as the consistency and quality of ink and quality of ink and of paper, the kind of pen used, and the position in which it is held, obviously condition line-quality. A very thick stroke points to materialism; while a writing in which there is no distinction of ground and hair stroke (the so-called "teigig" or "pâteuse" hand) indicates sensuality, a love of physical pleasures. The reason for connecting materialism with unusually heavy stroke is not given; it is, probably, purely analogical. Preyer states that the interpretation of the "teigig" hand is supported by experience but that the explanation is in doubt. The explanation sometimes suggested is that such a writing is produced by holding the pen at a very low angle with reference to the paper and that such holding of the pen is itself indicative of indolence and relaxation.

2. From the pathological standpoint we are told that variations in motor energy are reflected in thickness of strokes but in very different forms, depending upon pathological condition. Hyperkinesis produces, in general, "weighted" writing, the result of which is an increase in thickness of stroke. The pressure is often so great that the pen pierces the paper. When, however, speed passes a certain limit, such pressure is less evident.

Dimunition in energy of movement may have contradictory effects: it may result in writing that is abnormally heavy or in an excessively fine stroke. The former result appears when both reflex and voluntary reaction are enfeebled as in epilepsy; the latter when the psycho-motor inhibition affects voluntary contractions only, as in melancholia (**18:15, 89**). Variability in pressure may result from failure to graduate pressure in consequence of attention so enfeebled as to fail to distinguish between the principal and the accessory lines. (**18:89**)

Gross, from actual registration of pressure, reported subnormal pressure for the graphic movements of patients in the depressive period of circular insanity (**22:498**). In mania there appeared great fluctuations in pressure; often extreme pressure was associated with extreme speed and size as a manifestation of rising excitement. (**22:509**).

3. Osborn's discussion of line-quality and pressure is enlightening. Line-width is dependent to a great extent upon pen-position. A nearly vertical position gives a fine line of nearly uniform width without shading and with a tendency to a broken effect. It is usually associated with finger movement. A nearly horizontal position gives a broader line, with frequent shading, and is often associated with free arm movement. Pen position "can be determined by the location of the emphasis of shading." Because of variation in pen pressure on the nibs of the pen we get, when writing is viewed under the microscope, three classes of writers: "those who make the majority of pen strokes rougher on the left, on the right, or those whose strokes show uniformity—

right slant writing more frequently shows an excess of roughness on the right and lower side of pen strokes"—"The character and extent of the roughness of the line edges are greatly changed by changes in the character of the surface of the paper, in its sizing, and in the materials of which it is made. The result is also affected by the character and condition of the ink used and by the rapidity, direction, and weight of the stroke." (**36:131f.**)

The involuntary placing of emphasis is one of the most personal characteristics of writing and one that "almost baffles simulation." "The weight of hand, graduation of pressure, and placing of emphasis radically change the appearance of a writing as a whole without changing the form in any way," (**36**). There may result a hand that suggests strength, one that is the record of rapid, nervous movement shown in irregular broken lines; or one that shows in the heavy, ragged, uneven line lack of skill and constant variation in pressure. Pen pressure reveals the degree to which writing is free and unconscious or labored and halting.

4. In the experimental investigation of writing, distribution of pressure in graphic movements is one of the problems which has been attacked by the Kraepelinian methods. Gross reports a distinctive curve for every subject tested but warns the reader that this curve can be detected only by instrumental analysis. (**22:555**). Diehl reports that light pressure and high involuntary speed may coexist. For example, practice leads both to acceleration of graphic speed and decrease in pressure. VOLUNTARY increase of speed is accompanied by increased pressure. The relationship between speed and pressure is somewhat indirect; increase in pressure is due to increase of effort of will (Antrieb or Anregung); zeal for work is indicated by rising pressure (**13:51f**).

Hirt's investigations (**23a:370**) indicate that writing pressure obeys certain fundamental physiological and psychological laws. It increases (1) in a given direction of movement; (2) under influence of rhythmic tendencies;

(3) at conclusion of a series of movements (final emphasis). It is, however, impossible to determine variations in pressure from bare observation of writing-product. Only in part does it parallel thickness or width of line-stroke. Such divergence between actual pressure and line-quality is involved in the structure of the pen-point, since strokes which are perpendicular to the transverse of the nibs of the pen are necessarily heavier than those which parallel in direction the moving pen point, even though the pressure be the same in the two cases.

Apart from general laws governing pressure, individual differences are apparent in the distribution of pressure. Two main types are observable, correspondent to the motor and sensory reaction types. The first or motor type makes the writing movements in one impulse; the second, or sensory type, fractionate these movements. The impulses of the motor type are simpler, more continuous, more uncontrolled than those of the sensory type. The first make movements; the second, signs. Writing size, duration, speed, and pressure vary from one part of manuscript to another. At the beginning, writing is proportionately small, slow, and weak in pressure. As writing continues there is an increase to a maximum. Each line is a unit in itself as well as a part of a bigger whole. Fluctuations in pressure give evidence of renewed will-impulses. The attempt to produce writing of fine quality causes more than the usual fluctuation in speed, size, and pressure, for attention is on the form of the individual letter. Writing becomes more uniform in proportion as it is allowed to proceed automatically. **(23a:383)**

Meumann on the ground of difference in degree and distribution of pressure distinguishes three types of writing characteristic of men, women, and children respectively.

The concentration of attention upon writing movement causes an increase in pressure as is evident in disguised and retarded script, and, in general, increase in effort means increased pressure.

II Interpretation of Pressure or Line-Quality

GRAPHOLOGICAL	MECHANICAL	PATHOLOGICAL	EXPERIMENTAL
Symptomatic of qualities of will. Firm emphatic movements: strength of will. Club-shaped terminal strokes: forcefulness. Broad regular stroke: **persistence** of purpose. **Fluctuation in stroke;** vacillating **purpose.** **"Pateuse" script: sensuality.**	Writing material has much to do with line-quality. **Shading** depends upon pen-**position**, angle of pen to surface of paper, and direction of writing. **(Osborn.)** Gradation of **involuntary pressure is a personal characteristic of great constancy.**	Hyperexcitability may **lead** to such pressure **as** to pierce the paper. Great **fluctuations in** pressure appear in mania. Subnormal pressure **characterizes periods of depression.**	Distribution of pressure can be determined only from instrumental registration. Does not run parallel with shad**ing.** **A distinctive pressure-**curve exists for every individual, but can be deter**mined only by analysis of** writing movement. Pressure increases with **in-creased difficulty of task or** with *voluntary* increase **of** speed of writing. Heavy pressure frequently distinguishes retarded and disguised handwriting. With lightening of task pressure decreases. With growing expertness **and au-**tomatism, there is **decrease in pressure.** **In general, degree of pressure gives evidence of amount of effort.**

3. *Direction. A. Slant.*

1. The graphological interpretation of slant is pretty uniform. Slant to the right is natural and spontaneous. The degree of slant indicates impulsiveness, emotional susceptibility; the greater the slant the greater the emotivity. Vertical writing shows self-control, with the head ruling the heart. Back-slant is indicative of diffidence, reserve, a masking of the self, which may be carried so far that it shows disguise of the self, or even deceitfulness. Excessive slant to the right is found in the chirography of novelists, artists, and women. Verticality characterizes the writing of scientists and thinkers. Actors, diplomats, politicians may slant their writing to the left, and such slant may also be indicative of pathological hysterical tendencies or of criminal tendencies. Great variability in slant is thought to show variability of mood. Extreme right slant may indicate pathological lack of control.

Three suggestions are found in the literature of the subject as to the possible explanation of the correlation of slant with various emotional temperaments.

(a) Preyer's (**39**) explanation is the common one. Natural writing slants towards the right as shown by the reversion to such slant on the part of those taught a vertical system. Vertical and left-slanted writing demand more time and effort than natural writing and, therefore, indicate control and inhibition of natural impulses. Such writing is evidently self-conscious. Vertical writing may have been acquired during school years, but is usually replaced by a more rapid form of writing except in the case of those inhibited individuals who refuse to permit themselves to follow natural impulses and who continue to obey the compulsion of school or other authority. Back-slant is taught in no school and utilization of such an uncomfortable method of writing shows impulse toward concealment or repression, or it may indicate vanity.

(b) Schneidemühl (**42**) has recourse to the general principle of expression, namely, that friendly, objective interests are manifested by centrifugal outgoing gestures and attitude; and the erect, or withdrawn, posture is expressive of emotional withdrawal or reserve. In other words, slant to the right is likened to eccentric attitude or gesture; vertical or left slant to erect and concentric posture.

(c) Klages (**26a**) utilizes the principle of spatial Einfühlung in his characterological interpretation of slant. A natural slant to the right is not considered significant but the production of a vertical hand is held to be indicative of stability and self-control inasmuch as it reveals a feeling for space symbolism which associates fixity and self-mastery with erect position. Back slant is cited as a sign of extreme emotionalism with actual repression, rather than as an indication of extreme coldness of nature as many graphologists think.

The graphologists cite as evidence of their contention specimens of writing from persons of known characteristics. The prettiest bit of evidence is furnished by Preyer who claims that with advancing age and the loss of emotive susceptibility, writing formerly slanted shows a tendency to become vertical. His material included two thousand letters from his father which showed in their sequence an increasing verticality. Furthermore, Preyer cites a case of slant shifted towards verticality during a period of stress demanding self-control and concealment on the part of a young woman of his acquaintance, a verticality preceded and followed by slanted writing.

2. De Fursac tells us that slant is often modified in pathological writing, the normal inclination toward the right being replaced by vertical or back-slanting writing. Sometimes this modification is systematic; the patient seeks to disguise his hand or give it a touch of originality. At other times, generally when there is weakening of attention, such shifts in slant are transitory and casual. In general, slant is extremely variable in all conditions in which attention is profoundly disturbed. Great variability in slant from right to vertical and left is cited as characteristic of writing produced

in the post-paroxysms of epilepsy, and in the hyperkinetic state in manic-depressive insanity.

3. The handwriting expert (Osborn) reports that slant is very largely due to the system of writing that is learned originally. Moreover, such mechanical factors as the general position of the body with reference to the writing surface, the position of the paper on the table, and pen-position are influential. The graphologists recognize, of course, such factors but consider them accessory rather than basal. In this connection one may quote from Freeman (**16,d:130**) "Irregularities in slant are due to the fact that in making succeeding strokes the hand or arm is not in the same position. Sometimes the variations in position and the accompanying shifts in slant occur frequently and at irregular intervals; and sometimes the slant is uniform for a number of words, or even lines, and then there is a sudden change. There is also one other type of change in slant which is due, paradoxically, not to a change in the manner of holding the hand or arm but to the maintenance of the same position. This is the increased slant which occurs at the end of the line."

4. Considerable experimental work has been done on slant of writing. McAllister estimated from actual experiment the speed of movement in the different quadrants and found that movement to the right is more rapid than vertical writing and that left slant is slow and difficult. "Free full forearm movements in a horizontal plane are made more rapidly towards the body than away from it, up strokes taking more time than down strokes." (**45:76**) Overestimation of distances arises from increased muscular effort and irregularity of slant may grow out of conflict between eye and muscle sense.

Experimental graphology has shown that in attempts at disguise of writing, shift of slant is one of the first points of attack, the common shift being, of course, from right slant to a vertical or back-slant. In general, increase of attention to writing results in less slant from the vertical. Starch

(**43,a**) demonstrated that unconscious imitation operates to change slant when one is writing from a copy.

It would seem as though evidence were pretty complete that vertical writing, print, and back-hand are slower (Note), less natural and comfortable than a slant toward the right. Verticality and back-slant indicate greater motor tension, greater conscious control, with evidence of inhibition. So much is plain. The real question is why anyone writes these hands when he might embrace the greater graphic comfort of a natural hand. Vertical writing has, of course, been taught at various times. It is, also, the accepted style for certain professions. But the natural inclination for those who have acquired a vertical hand is to modify it as soon as pressure is released. Retention of vertical habit would evidence a conventional, controlled type of person who follows the prescribed path. Occasionally, vertical script might be adopted by one who had been otherwise taught, through an impulse to imitate or because its legibility makes strong appeal. Whether verticality is ever adopted because of spatial symbolism is an interesting question but one not easily answered.

Why, however, does anyone write the awkward and uncomfortable backslant? This style is taught in no school and is advocated by no system of writing. It might originate, of course, through imitation and quite possibly it may be at times expressive of affectation and self-consciousness. But that these explanations are not sufficient in all cases is evident from reports from individuals who write a reversed hand. Quite often they report that they deliberately adopted this hand to relieve the strain experienced when writing a more usual type of script.

Another factor in its production, which has never been sufficiently canvassed, is its relation to ambidextral tendencies. Definitely left-handed persons often write very fluent

NOTE—The investigation of Graves (loc. cit. p. 490) does not confirm this statement so far as back-hand is concerned. He found back-hand most rapid but least staple of all slants.

right-slanted script, but shiftovers who have been compelled to change from the major to the minor hand, and those with a tendency to ambidextrality show signs of lack of smooth coordination in writing or have recourse to a drawing movement which results in print instead of cursive script. Sometimes the ambidexter indulges in reversed script. In a number of instances I have experimental evidence of ambidextral tendencies in the writers of a back-hand. Furthermore, in connection with measurements on bone lengths of right and left arm, I found that of fourteen individuals whose measurements gave little difference in bone-length for the two arms, five wrote either a completely reversed hand or gave numerous reversals of slant. Two others, who wrote a reversed hand, gave only a moderate difference in arm measurement. I have never found but one individual writing reversed script who proved by tests to be very strongly unidextral.

It is difficult to make any connection between such observations as the preceding, and the teaching of the graphologists. Yet a connection is possible provided that unidextrality and ambidextrality are correlated with different temperamental types, which correlation if found to be a fact would find its ultimate explanation in the somewhat different functioning of the nervous system in the two instances.

Interpretation of Slant

GRAPHOLOGICAL	MECHANICAL	PATHOLOGICAL	EXPERIMENTAL
Symptomatic of affective qualities. Extreme slant to right: emotional susceptibility, impulsiveness, irritability. Verticality: self-control, reserve. Left slant: power of concealment, repression or emotional coldness. Fluctuations in slant: variability in emotional reactions.	Largely determined by system of writing learned, modified by different form of movement and by position of paper on table. General position of body with reference to writing surface important. Shift of slant in line due to varying position of hand. Irregularity in slant due to conflict of visual and muscular sensations.	Extremely variable in all states where attention is disturbed. Unstable.	Natural slant toward the right. With release of motor impulse increased slant: with inhibition, increased steepness. Attention to writing results in greater verticality. Slant easily modified voluntarily. Unconscious imitation operates to change slant. In disguised writing common shift is toward vertical or backhand. Spontaneous back-slant may be due to ambidextral tendencies. A mixed slant shows instability; it is particularly noticeable at beginning of adolescent period. (Graves.)

B. Alignment.

1. Variations in alignment are also correlated by the graphologists with general temperamental traits or with emotional fluctuations. Rising alignment indicates optimism, self-confidence, or ambition: falling alignment, pessimism, depression mediated by outer conditions, or sickness. Convexity and concavity of line indicate waxing and waning ardor, that fluctuates as work proceeds. Serpentine lines evidence suppleness of mind, skill in finesse, falsity; serpentine words, quick sensibility, agitation, nervousness.

Modifications of these traditional interpretations appear in the standard texts. Preyer, for example, fails to find serpentine alignment in the writing of many clever politicians and diplomatists and, on the other hand, discovers it in the writing of many persons who are totally devoid of such a make-up. Nor does Preyer find straight alignment correlated with equability of temperament.

The explanation suggested for the graphological interpretation is that of emotional mimicry. In joyous excitement there is an inclination to raise the arms upward, in general, to aspire. The sad let the arms fall. But Preyer observes: "These and also many other mimicry signs have only a superficial analogy." (**39:185**) He also calls attention to the fact that what in writing is called upward or downward alignment is in reality centrifugal or centripetal movement; only when writing on a vertical surface do we actually get rising or falling movement. Preyer accepts, largely on empirical grounds, the traditional assertion concerning rising and falling alignment and instances differences in alignment in a letter of condolence from that in a letter of congratulation.

The bar of the "t" furnishes another example of alignment, and the interpretation of an up-stroke, a down-stroke, a serpentine stroke and the like is the same as for direction of line of writing. In this instance, however, alignment is complicated with variations in extent and force of stroke.

2. DeFursac, commenting on alignment in pathological writing, remarks that one might expect that pathological conditions would have the same graphic expression as the correspondent normal states, that in the maniac pride and self-exaltation would produce rising lines and that humility and discouragement would in the melancholic produce falling alignment. Unfortunately the case is not so simple. It is, he asserts, impossible in the present state of our knowledge to determine any constant or necessary relation between alignment and mental disturbances. **(18)** The following observations are, however, justified:

(1) Undulating lines are significant from the motor side of incoordination of movements and from the psychic side of feebleness of attention.

(2) Falling alignment is seen often (but not always) in conditions of motor weakness, in particular in the post-paroxysmal exhaustion of epilepsy.

(3) Rising alignment appears in the writing of certain patients who through lack of initiative fail to give their paper the desired inclination and permit their hand to move in an automatic fashion. Rising alignment in such a case is usually combined with a curved form of the line.

(4) The curved form of the line is associated with the undulating in certain maladies that are characterized by automatic reactions, notably in the case of the catatonics. The forearm remains immobile; the hand moves around the wrist as a center. **(18:11f.)**

Specifically, in general paralysis lines are often more or less undulating, due both to enfeeblement of attention and motor incoordination. Falling alignment frequently occurs in melancholic and depressive forms of nervous disease but there is no fixed rule. In dementia precox, the direction of lines varies from a perfect horizontal in some to a rising or falling alignment in other cases without any possibility of establishing a relationship between the direction of alignment and the clinic character of the disease. **(18:147)**

In manic excitement, also, there is no constant relationship of alignment. Rising alignment occurs but so also does horizontal and falling alignment (**18:197**), a statement which also holds true for melancholic depressive insanity. (**18:211**)

3. Osborn finds that alignment is largely the result of pivotage of movement. The writing of the illiterate usually shows an up-hill tendency. The "arm is so held that the center of motion is so far to the right that as the hand moves along it is inevitably raised above the general line of writing." (**36:121**) Perfect alignment results when the elbow is the center of lateral movement and the arm at right angles to the line of writing. With the wrist as center of motion there may result lines of writing equal to short arcs of a circle representing the reach of the hand with the wrist at rest. Most uneven alignment is due to the fact that the arm is too far around to the right or the paper too far to the left. Deviation from alignment in individual letters is often due to the design of letter acquired when writing was first learned.

4. From the experimental side there is little to report. It would appear from Woodworth' experiments (**48**) that vision functions somewhat in control of alignment and results obtained from writing when the eyes are blindfolded confirm his conclusions. Often a loss of alignment is the only noticeable result with loss of visual control.

Writing disguise affords little material so far as alignment is concerned. Alignment is an exceedingly variable element and one which can be manipulated with ease. It would, perhaps, seem on general principles that falling alignment might be cited as evidence of inhibitory tendencies and Klages in fact lists falling alignment as one characteristic of the inhibited hand. In experiments of my own on retarded writing a decided fall in direction appears as one outcome of excessive control.

The assertion is frequently encountered in the literature of experimental graphology that the contents of an emotional letter or other manuscript influence alignment. Such reports are of little import in the form in which they are given for there is no narration of the conditions under which such observations were made. Comparison of alignment in epistles of contrasting emotional content emanating from different penmen is of dubious value unless one have, also, specimens of the normal writing of each. In this instance intra-individual variability under prescribed conditions is the point at issue rather than inter-individual variability. The problem is a difficult one to attack experimentally since it is not an easy matter to tap emotion for experimental purposes.

I have tried the following test. First, I obtained from a number of subjects specimens of their normal writing on the blackboard and determined the error in alignment. Then at short intervals I have had memorized and written sentences of two or more lines each (1) prophesying a gloomy outcome of the world war; (2) suggesting encouraging prospects in the war situation; and (3) commenting on certain amusing aspects of food conservation. Precautions were taken that the first and second sentences should be written at the same height and relative position on the board and that the lines should be approximately of the same length (one meter). Using the natural writing as the standard of comparison (in every case there was falling alignment) I found that out of fifteen items (three averages each for five subjects) the gloomy content resulted in an increased fall in alignment twice out of a possible five times; the cheerful content in a decreased fall in direction or even in rising alignment seven times out of a possible ten. The subjects were, of course, absolutely unaware of the purpose of the test. They were adults seriously interested in the war conditions.

A somewhat similar experiment with students, but less satisfactorily controlled, gave increased fall with gloomy content three times out of a possible four and one rise in the contrasting test out of a possible six. Such results are inconclusive.

In Part II, observations are reported on variability in slant and alignment under normal changes in mood. Anticipating conclusions, I may say here that there was some evidence of increased slant and unstable alignment under heightened emotional conditions but that these modifications were so deeply embedded in general slant and line variability as to make practical utilization very uncertain. Results suggest de Fursac's report with reference to alignment in pathological writing. Under hyperkinetic and hypokinetic conditions alignment departs from the horizontal but with little consistency as regards direction. Rising, falling and undulating lines are recorded.

Interpretation of Alignment

GRAPHOLOGICAL	MECHANICAL	PATHOLOGICAL	EXPERIMENTAL
Symptomatic of temperamental qualities. Rising alignment: optimism, ambition, pride. Falling alignment: pessimism, humility, discouragement. Straight alignment: equability. Sinuous alignment: suppleness of spirit. Convex and concave lines: vacillating attitude. Rising alignment may indicate irritability or restlessness.	Alignment largely a matter of pivotage of movements. With elbow as center of lateral movement and arm at right angles to line of writing perfect alignment results. Shifts in alignment due mainly to differences in movements, position of paper (?) and design of letters. Angle of paper important.	No constant relation between nature of malady and direction of line. Rising alignment appears in writing of patients who, through lack of initiative, neglect giving their paper the desired inclination. Falling alignment occurs often in conditions of motor enfeeblement. Undulating alignment indicates motor incoordination or feebleness of attention. The automatic reactions of the catatonic result in short curves executed with the wrist as a center	Vision is concerned in maintaining alignment. Writing with eyes closed results in all manner of errors in alignment. Preyer asserts that content affects alignment.

4. *Continuity.*

1. The traditional interpretation of the graphic sign that we may call continuity, or the degree to which letters are connected within words, is that connected script is symptomatic of a deductive habit of thought, and a broken or disconnected hand of an inductive habit of thinking.

Careful reading, however, indicates that the terms inductive and deductive are not to be interpreted in the technical sense in which they are used in logic. The adjective "deductive" seems to imply a practical realistic type of mind in contrast to a visionary theoretical type. The " deductive" thinker does not originate ideas but is thoroughly well able to assimilate and turn to good account the ideas of others; he exhibits a high degree of practical judgment and is interested in application. In general, he may be described as reasonable, systematic, methodical, and prosaic. The "inductive" thinker produces original ideas which are the outcome of his intuitions and his lively imagination; he is theoretical rather than practical, visionary rather than logical. His feelings overbalance his judgment.

Preyer (**39:138f**) gives us a fivefold division of hands on the basis of degree of connectedness as follows: (a) Pure "intuitive" hand, every letter detached, breaks sometimes occurring within letters; symptomatic of originality, fertility of thought, one interrupting another; no time taken to follow any to their logical consequences. Cited as the handwriting of such men as Chateaubriand, Victor Hugo, Mazzini, Verdi. (b) The hand that is more intuitive than deductive, symptomatic of a mind that is productive of new ideas, reasonable or not, with greater inclination to follow now one idea now another than to compare ideas in a logical manner. (c) Equal number of united and disconnected letters, symptomatic of possession of new ideas and capacity to unite them logically; union of idealism and realism; enthusiasm for the new and appreciation for the old; union of judgment and imagination; balanced intellectual type. Within this group, however, there appears a subgroup in which the breaks within words occur in an illogical manner separating the words into bizarre combinations of letters, a trait which is cited as significant of impracticality. (d) If the hand is primarily a continuous one with few breaks, the penman is thought to possess the gift of synthesis with capacity for proper appreciation of new ideas. This is the writing of scientists and statesmen who excel in organization, but are accessible to new ideas. (e) The completely continuous hand, every word written without raising of pen, words bound together by the stroke of the "t" and the like, is thought to characterize the hand of the assimilative type who is neither critical, original, nor ingenious.

Schneidemühl, who cites this interpretation from Preyer, accepts it only with considerable reserve since his own observations fail frequently to confirm it. This much, however, he concedes, that the writer of the "deductive" hand coordinates and renders coherent the material with which he deals.

Preyer's ground for such characterological interpretation would appear to be empirical, just as Schneidemühl's dissent is based on specific observations. I have found in these authors no psychological ground for their interpretation.

Crépieux-Jamin cites the "hachée" hand as indicative of intuition but also on occasion as evidencing anguish, or circulatory troubles. The connected hand he finds significant of natural activity and of culture, or of precipitation and flight of ideas.

2. Turning now to de Fursac's treatment of graphic continuity, we find that disconnected or even "hachée" script is found, on the one hand, when movements are hesitant or deprived of regularity and harmony, particularly in patients who are afflicted with trembling, and, on the other hand, when attention is profoundly disturbed. When associated with tremor, discontinuity may be the natural outcome of an attempt at simplification of movement. Script very much tied together is often produced under conditions of extreme excitement. Not only the letters of the same word but the

words themselves are joined. This tying together of words may be the outcome of excessive rapidity. But pathological writing shows no greater extremes of continuity and discontinuity than does normal writing. (**18:28**)

A more or less connected script instead of broken writing may occur in conditions of depression and motor enfeeblement, in which case failure to raise the pen is due to lack of energy sufficient to accomplish this movement. Sometimes in very great affective melancholia the pen loses contact with the paper and causes a break even within letters. (**18:221; 213**)

3. For the handwriting expert the degree of continuity is largely a matter of expertness. Osborn writes: "With those who write clumsily or with difficulty the pen is raised frequently to get a new adjustment—with most writers, however, disconnections are more closely related to design of letters than with movement, and the habit controlling this characteristic were acquired when writing was first learned." (**36:121**)

4. From the experimental side there is little one can say about continuity. There is plenty of evidence to show that, in part at least, a flowing connected hand is the outcome of graphic expertness. Many breaks in writing may be significant of nothing more than graphic unaccustomedness. Klages shows, further, that breaks in writing may result from motor inhibition and from excessive attention to writing. This appears from study of disguised and artificial writing. One may, voluntarily, introduce breaks into writing but it is impossible to will extreme continuity. Release of the motor impulse causes increased continuity; while inhibition results in decreased continuity.

It is difficult to see any connection whatever between these last observations and the traditional interpretation by graphologists of the significance of graphic continuity. The only possibility of alliance would be found in the determination of a possible relationship between attention types and a connected or disconnected hand.

Interpretation of Continuity

GRAPHOLOGICAL	MECHANICAL	PATHOLOGICAL	EXPERIMENTAL
Symptomatic of logical and imaginative qualities of mind. Connected writing: deductive, rationative, practical, organizing type of mind. Broken writing: inductive intuitive, theoretical, idealistic type of mind.	"With those who write clumsily or with difficulty the pen is raised frequently to get a new adjustment. With most writers, however, these connections are more closely related to design of letters than with movement, and the habits controlling this characteristic were acquired when writing was first learned." (Osborn.)	So variable an element that it is difficult to determine its pathological modifications.	Extreme continuity more difficult to will than extreme discontinuity. With release of motor impulse increased continuity. Attention to writing results in decreased continuity. In disguised writing more breaks occur than in natural writing. Extreme continuity, a sign of graphic expertness and speed.

5. *Proportion above and below the base line.*

1. The authorities are somewhat at odds in their interpretation of the significance of relative proportion of strokes above and below the base line. Two traditional views emphasize two related but somewhat distinct interpretations. A long up-stroke is correlated by the first with predisposition for mental activity and a long down-stroke with a predisposition for physical activity. The second point of view states that the long up-stroke signifies idealistic make-up, impractical and out of touch with reality (the real world); and the long down-stroke preoccupation with things material. Balanced proportion denotes power of organization and administration.

Both Preyer and Schneidemühl are sceptical of the traditional beliefs. Preyer finds in his collection of specimens numerous examples of short upstrokes among penmen following intellectual pursuits from motives distinctly not materialistic. He has, however, more faith in the deduction of lack of foresight and circumspection from very short, incomplete, and attached down-strokes. Schneidemühl from his study of specimens is inclined, on empirical grounds only, to assert a correlation of decreased down-stroke with impracticality, lack of foresight, irresolution, and failure in the execution of details. Normal extension above and below the base-line seems symptomatic of practical sense. He cautions, however, conservatism in such application and notes that there has as yet been no psychological grounding suggested for such an interpretation.

2. Pathological writing affords little information concerning the trait in question. One outcome of a hyperkinetic condition appears, however, in exaggeration of terminal loops, of capitals, and in excessive prolongation of movements of adduction.

3. In the general analysis of graphic elements by the expert, relative proportion is cited as very simply dependent upon the system of writing learned. The Spencerian system was organized on a scale of fifths; the vertical system

in thirds. Prior to the adoption of modern Spencerian, other proportions existed in relative height of small and loop letters.

4. Some experimental work has been done on ease of movement relative to the body as a center. McAllister found that "Free, full forearm movements in a horizontal plane are made more rapidly towards the body than away from it, up strokes taking more time than down strokes." (**45:76**)

In disguised handwriting we find considerable attention given to relative proportion as of considerable importance in identification of a hand. While changes in absolute size are very easily produced voluntarily, certain changes in relative proportion are maintained only with the greatest difficulty; increase in the length of the up-strokes, for example. Increase in length of the down-strokes, particularly in terminal loops, may, however, be imitated with considerable ease.

Hands vary considerably in amount of difference in extension of small and lower loop letters. Very extreme inequality is usually found in minute writing, an inequality which Klages (**26:37f**) considers evidence of the presence of strong inhibitory impulses which operate in keeping the minimum letters small. Very long "long" letters in small script are interpreted as the outcome of intermittent freeing of the motor impulse. From Klages' standpoint it is possible to make a connection between lack of circumspection and the short down-stroke.

INTERPRETATION OF PROPORTION

GRAPHOLOGICAL	MECHANICAL	PATHOLOGICAL	EXPERIMENTAL
Variation in interpretation. Traditional views: (1) long up-stroke, mental activity; long down-stroke, physical activity, or (2) long up-stroke, idealistic proclivities; long down-stroke, materialistic ones. Short down-strokes may indicate lack of practicality, of foresight and of circumspection.	Dependent upon writing system. Spencerian system organized in fifths; vertical, in thirds. Greater inequality in certain earlier systems.	Increase in adductive movement in hyperkinetic conditions.	Relative proportions of letters and letter-parts constant characteristic of a hand. Very difficult to change deliberately. Hence this feature is much used in identification of writing.

The preceding survey impresses one with the difficulties that must be compassed by a scientific graphology. It suggests a program for preliminary exploration that is overwhelming. Any attempt at present to utilize graphic products in psychodiagnosis would seem futile except that in many instances a variation which in itself has little significance acquires such through its association with other signs which suggest the same motor pattern. It would seem possible to detect in certain hands signs of inhibition, control or retardation. Slow and interrupted movement, small size, vertical or back-slant, great inequality in length, and unevenness or heaviness of pressure point to inhibitory tendencies. Light rapid continuous rhythmic hands, slanted strongly in the direction of writing, evidence lack of inhibition. It is, of course, possible to grant so much and yet deny all characterological significance. Graphic habits acquired in youth may be sufficient to account for the free or inhibited pattern. But that habit is not all-sufficient as an explanation seems evident from the following. Pathological writing under prescribed conditions exhibits in the hyperkinetic hand an exaggeration of the explosive or free hand. Moreover, the changes introduced into the writing of a given individual under conditions of increased control or mental effort encourage the interpretation of certain signs as symptomatic of control and effort in general. In Part II, we shall report a number of experiments that bear upon an attempt to interpret the significance of explosive and inhibited hands.

Part II

CHAPTER V.

DISGUISED HANDWRITING.

In our previous discussions we have had frequent occasion to refer to the significance of handwriting disguise. Let us now envisage the subject at closer quarters.

The determination of the extent to which handwriting may be disguised is a problem of considerable importance from at least two points of view. On the one hand, as a practical problem, of great interest from the legal standpoint, it arises in connection with the imitation of the writing of others in forgeries that are not traceries and in the "masked" writing of the anonymous letter. On the other hand, from the psychological or theoretical side, the range and method of handwriting disguise is, as we have seen, of significance in connection with the utilization of handwriting in psychodiagnosis.

Our concern is, of course, with the second of these two considerations. In passing, however, it should be observed that the handwriting experts have much to say concerning the difficulties involved in the identification of handwriting and the determination of the original of a disguised hand. They insist upon the need of cautious procedure; they list the sources of possible error; and they warn against the acceptance of the unsupported opinion of the incompetent and untrained witness. Mr. Osborn writes, (**36;c**) "There are two main questions that confront the examiner of an alleged forgery. The first of these is how much and to what extent may a genuine writing diverge from a certain type, and the second is how and to what extent will a more or less skillful forgery be likely to succeed and be likely to fail in embodying the characteristics of a genuine writing." These two questions (1) of the limits of variation in a natural hand and (2) of the graphic characteristics that may or may not be easily assumed are of first importance from the theoretical side also.

A significant item of difference between the emphasis of the handwriting expert and that of the psychologist should, however, be noted. The expert approaches the problem largely from the standpoint of the degree of credibility of the witness testifying in court concerning the genuineness of handwriting. The psychologist would press the matter further back and determine, if possible, the reason for the great individual differences that exist, apart from training, with respect to observation of handwriting individuality. Furthermore, he is most curious concerning the varying capacity for disguise exhibited by different penmen and the mental temperament that lies back of virtuosity in the assumption of different handwriting individualities. Lastly, he would ask what the psycho-physical factors are that determine the ease or difficulty with which different graphic elements may be voluntarily altered.

The problem of control in handwriting, which we have emphasized as a basal one so far as psychodiagnosis is concerned, centers about two problems both of which are open to experimentation: (1) The extent to which disguise of one's habitual handwriting is possible and (2) the extent to which voluntary control is maintained in conventional writing as evidenced by the changes that take place in automatic writing or writing under distraction. In everyday life an obvious indication of this latter change is the difference between writing furbished up for state occasions and writing designed for domestic purposes, in negligee so to speak. In ordinary writing, control becomes progressively less rigid as one becomes interested in the content of what he is writing or as speed of writing increases. The first half of each word, the first half of a written line, and of a manuscript give evidence of greater control than does the second half. The significance of this variation in conscious control, so often emphasized by graphologists, need not detain us here. Instead let us turn to the problem of voluntary disguise of *handwriting*.

For scientific purposes one strikes the problem at close quarters by an experimental treatment such, for instance, as that of Dr. George Meyer. (**34a**) Meyer approached the question from four different angles: (1) Which graphic characters can be *repressed* voluntarily? (2) Which can be assumed *voluntarily?* (3) What is the result of a deliberate attempt to disguise handwriting? (4) How far is imitation of another hand possible?

To obtain an answer to question 1, a large number of subjects were asked to write as calligraphically as possible, in true copy-book style of the school-room. Normals were also obtained for comparison. To obtain an answer to question 2, definite variations in particular graphic characters were asked for from twenty-five different reagents. Question 3 was answered by asking subjects to disguise their writing; question 4 by asking for imitation of specific hands. From his study of the methods of intentional disguise employed by unsophisticated subjects, Meyer was able to draw some interesting conclusions concerning the graphic elements that are least subject to control, which in the main are precisely those to which the average observer pays least attention.

I have notes on an experiment of my own similar in purpose to that of Meyer but developed in a somewhat different manner.

I asked twenty-four unsophisticated subjects to write a given verse on an unlined sheet of standard size and quality in their usual manner. I then requested each of them to rewrite this verse on a second similar sheet but disguising their handwriting as far as possible. No instructions were given as to method of disguise. Each subject could take all the time and pains that he cared to in the disguise, which was prepared *away* from the laboratory. In selecting my subjects I chose twelve of each sex. With reference to age they fell into two groups also, twelve under twenty-six years of age and twelve over thirty. The younger group was, with one exception, composed of college students; the older group, with three exceptions, of University instructors, Four of the latter were psychologists. Such a selection of subjects was dictated by a desire to see whether age and sex were factors governing success in disguise. The degree to which a given disguise was held to be successful was determined by the submission of the series of disguised and undisguised writings to sixteen reagents for matching and the counting of the number of times a disguised specimen was correctly matched with the undisguised specimen written by the same penman.

The material obtained in this manner was worked over with the following questions in mind: (1) What methods of disguise were utilized by the group of subjects? (2) To what extent were the individual attempts at disguise effective as determined by the percentage of failures on the part of the judges in identification of the disguised hand? Were the younger penmen more successful than the older ones in disguise? Was there any difference in the percentage of successes of men and women?

In an attempt to answer the first question, out of almost numberless observations that might be made relative to changes in the graphic characters, tabulation was limited to the obvious shifts in size, slant, pressure or line-quality, form, continuity, alignment, connecting-stroke, relative proportion, and i-dot. See Table 1.

TABLE I

METHODS UTILIZED IN DISGUISE OF WRITING BY 24 SUBJECTS

Number of Times There Was a Noticeable Shift In

Size, 17	Slant, 16	Pressure, 15	Form, 16	Alignment 16	Continuity 11	Connecting-stroke, 17	Proportion, 16	i-dot, 5
Decreased 11	To back-hand or vertical 15	Increased 12	Ornamented 8	Straightened 6	Decreased 8	More rounded 12	One space letter 7	Change in form 5
Increased 6	To right 1	Decreased 3	Fantastic 2	More serpentine 4	Increase 3	More angular 5	Increased down stroke 5	In localization ?
			Simplified 6	Rising 4			Decreased down stroke 2	
				Falling 2			Increased up stroke 2	

A word of comment upon each of these chosen elements is desirable. A change in size of writing is a frequent outcome of disguise, a decrease being more common than an increase in size of letters. There is, in fact, in the given specimens no case of increased size comparable to the extremes of decrease. The decrease in size of letters is usually accompanied by greater compactness in texture leading to a compression in the horizontal extension. This same compression appears also in a few cases in which the writing is increased in size but, usually, increased amplitude is accompanied by a looser texture.

A shift in slant was also noticeable in the disguised hand, usually in the direction of the vertical or backhand. Such a change is one that readily appeals to the unsophisticated, although handwriting individuality is but little dependent upon slant of writing.

The degree to which pressure varied in the natural and the disguised hand cannot be told with any degree of accuracy from the written product. Experiments on pressure demand, as we have seen, actual instrumental registration. Certain changes in line-quality were, however, very evident in a large number of cases. In a majority of specimens this change is in the direction of a heavier line. I do not find, unfortunately, a record of how many of my subjects used a different style of pen in attempting to disguise their hands, but in any case it is unlikely that such a shift accounts for the uniformity in direction of change.

In consideration of variations in letter-form, the writing-specimen was scrutinized to determine whether on the whole there was simplification or conventionalizing of the natural hand or whether the reagent attempted to disguise his hand by the employment of superfluous ornamentation or fantastic forms. Recourse to a conventional vertical hand or to print is one of the most effective means of disguise but it is more difficult to achieve than a hand decked out with all manner of superfluous curls. It demands more consistent motor control. The tabulation given overlooks the many details of form that would be so carefully noted by the expert in attempting to prove or disprove the genuineness of a given writing. Individual mannerisms, tricks of style, are often revealed in the form of individual letters and one of the most interesting questions involved in disguised handwriting is the extent to which a penman is aware of his individual peculiarities and the consistency with which he is able to avoid tell-tale mannerisms. Such observation does not, however, lend itself to tabulation. Changes in capitals are more easily achieved than changes in small letters; they are made with a higher degree of consciousness.

A change in alignment occurs frequently but without much uniformity as to the direction.

The degree of continuity in a given hand is one of its most distinctive marks. This character is held to be very largely dependent upon the general smoothness and regularity of the motor impulse, a matter, to a considerable degree, of the original constitution. A break in continuity is much more easily initiated than is increased continuity, as a simple outcome of intentional inhibition. It is a much more difficult matter to release deliberately the motor impulse and so increase the degree of continuity.

Changes in the form of the connecting stroke occur frequently, more commonly from an angular to a rounded connection than the reverse.

While the absolute size of writing is easily shifted, relative proportion of parts is pretty constant. The latter depends upon periodicity of effort which is rooted in constitutional rhythm. There are, however, a very great number of possible observations relative to proportion, among them the following: Relative proportion of strokes above and below the line, relative size of one-space and three-space letters, relative horizontal and vertical space relations of the one-space letters, relative proportion of capital and strokes above the line. It is much more difficult to vary some of these proportions than others. For example, from my results, it appears that a change in the relative size of the one-space letters is not infrequent, while changes in the relative proportions of up and down strokes is less often observed. An increase in the relative length of an up-stroke is said to be particularly difficult to achieve, and my specimens show only two cases in which such a change was evident. An increase in the relative length of a down-stroke is much more common, and, in general, an increase in difference in length is twice as frequent as a decrease in difference in length.

The mannerisms exhibited in dotting the "i" are very constant. This i-dot may be observed from three points of view; its localization, that is, the distance it is placed above the line and its position directly above or to the right or the left of the "i"; secondly, its form, which varies in an extraordinary number of ways from comma-shaped to wedge-shaped, not to mention its size; and, thirdly, the time of its making, immediately after the letter itself or after the word or line has been written. One would need to watch the penman while writing in order to establish this latter habit. In the disguises I collected, there are no obvious changes of localization in the placing of the dot, although in several specimens there is great variability in the natural hand itself. So far as form was concerned there were several deliberate attempts to vary it. Bizarre substitutions were adopted, such as the circle, or a v-shaped figure. I am inclined to think that two or three of these changes were motivated by a knowledge on the part of the penman of the fact that the dot of an "i" is most characteristic.

Some of the changes just mentioned are deliberate, a revelation of what the subject believes to be characteristic of handwriting. The more constant a mark, the less conscious awareness of it. Of these deliberately sought shifts, some are easily manipulated, slant, for example, and change in absolute size. Others are handled with greater difficulty because of their dependence upon psycho-physical factors, as, for instance, degree of connection. Still other changes are dependent upon the general instruction to disguise the hand and are not directly willed by the subject nor even noticed by him. Such are the three general symptoms of disguise: (1) Instability, (2) Signs of Tension, and (3) Inner Contradiction.

Let us be more specific. Absolute size is easily changed voluntarily. But not all changes in size are to be attributed to direct volition. Increased attention to writing results in decrease in the size of writing and in increased pressure. The uniformity with which changes occurred in these directions is, then, in part at least, an outcome of effort of attention and not wholly a product of intention. Increased size, on the other hand, may result from discontinuity of the motor impulse so that each letter is written as a separate unit rather than as part of a word. One would expect to find this increase in size in disguises in which attention is concentrated upon variation in the form of individual letters. Frequently, breaks in connection between letters would also result from such a break-up of the motor impulse.

Alignment and the shape of the i-dot may be deliberately varied if one chance to know his own mannerisms and if he can hold his attention consistently to the detail in question. Details of form are very hard to change, particularly in the middle and at the end of a word. The style of a capital is not hard to shift.

The results of this canvass of the methods utilized in disguise of hands agree very closely with what has been reported by Meyer as the outcome of his investigation and with the scheme adopted by the Berlin police in their indexing of handwriting specimens as part of their system of identification of criminals. In this latter system the characteristics of handwriting are arranged in a descending scale beginning with the elements that are most easily altered and ending with those that are least subject to change.

The order is as follows (**26a**):

Size
Pressure
Emphasis of the under stroke
Ataxia (unformed and trembling writing)

Verticality
Compression
Slant
Width
Increase in proportional length
Simplification
Ornamentation
Disconnection
Connection
Emphasis of the upper stroke
Form of the connecting stroke
Decrease in proportional length
Change in single forms

A further point of interest is a comparison of these shifts that accompany an effort to disguise the hand, with concentration of attention upon the act of writing, with those that are the outcome of distraction of attention from writing and, in some instances, of completely automatic writing. The shift in size that is significant of automatic writing has been somewhat thoroughly discussed in another connection (**14a**). Increase in size is a general outcome of increased automatism, just as decrease in size is an effect of concentration of attention upon writing, unless the latter result in a complete dissociation of letters and a distinct motor impulse for each. A decrease in pressure is also an outcome of automatic writing but less evidently so than the increase in size. Completely automatic writing results apparently in script that is more continuous than the usual writing but in case of incomplete distraction there would be alternate fixation and release of attention with, probably, increased discontinuity. Changes in slant do not occur in automatic writing as they do in disguised hands, although there seems to be in some cases a tendency to greater verticality. Changes in form are in the direction of disorganized or child-like hands.

Between the two extremes of voluntarily disguised writing and writing produced without conscious supervision lies the ordinary writing with which graphology deals. It is evident where one should look for lapse of control. Periodic fluctuation of attention enables us to anticipate the fall of the mask at various points. In ordinary writing there is heightened consciousness and hence greater control (1) at the beginning of the activity, inscribing, for example, the first page of a manuscript, the first word of a line, etc.; (2) after interruption of the writing activity by paragraphing or punctuation marks; (3) at variation in the form of the activity such as the production of capitals. Controlled writing is smaller, more vertical, and more regular than uncontrolled writing, that is, the same signs appear as in disguised writing but in less pronounced form. Conventional restraint becomes progressively difficult as speed of writing increases. With deepening interest in content, writing becomes freer and bolder. Every prolonged piece of writing shows the shift from conscious to involuntary control, and in this fact the graphologist finds an opportunity for observation of certain characteristics of the motor impulse.

Let us turn now to the second question, the success of a disguise as determined by the failure of the judges in penetration of the disguise.

But before entering upon the question of the success of the individual penman, a word concerning the varying skill of the sixteen judges. The range in success runs from only one correct identification of the twenty-four specimens of disguised hands to an accurate pairing of eleven specimens (a record made by a bank cashier). The average number of correct identifications (and the median record) is six, or twenty-five per cent.

About half of the judges were taken from the college community which produced the disguised hands, and, in some cases, they recognized a number of the natural hands. This familiarity with the natural hand increased slightly the number of correct identifications. There exists, however, a very great individual difference in the ease with which handwriting is recognized even when undisguised and in the facility with which handwriting specimens by the same penman may be paired. For ten of my judges in this test I have record of their success in the matching of undisguised hands. The group is too small to be of much value but the results of the two tests give a positive coefficient of correlation of .41 (P. E., .18).

The outcome of this aspect of the experiment justifies the distrust on the part of the most careful handwriting experts of the opinion of the ordinary observer as to the genuineness of a given hand. The chance of error is so great that the judgment of the amateur can have little weight, although, obviously, the opinion of one may be worth more than that of another,—a matter which could be determined only by a controlled test. Certainly the confidence with which a witness—or a reagent in the psychological experiment—expresses his opinion bears little relation to his value as an observer and might be most misleading in a trial in court.

Such strictures against handwriting-identification on the part of the amateur only serve to point the value of the work of the expert, with his instruments of precision, his microscope, his enlarged photographs, his multiplication of observations, and his knowledge of where to look for significant variations.

Three of the judges who took part in the test on disguised handwriting were given a second trial at matching after an explanation had been given them concerning the significant features of writing individuality. They were advised to ignore changes in size, slant, and form of capitals. Their increased success was as follows: (A) from nine to twelve correct identifications; (B) from six to nine; (C) from five to eight.

So far as the individual disguises are concerned, some were much more effective than others. Three hands could scarcely be called disguised since they were correctly paired by almost every judge. Of the other twenty-one, four were so well disguised as to wholly elude capture. Eight were identified by only one or two judges each.

The three who fail completely at disguise write very individual hands. Their failure was evident to themselves and they made subsequent attempts to mask their writing without much greater success. Of the four completely successful disguises, one is a semi-print style; another is a most clever imitation of a friend's hand included among the specimens, with which it is matched by four different judges. Two others show very great shifts in slant and size, changes which however easily manipulated seem quite effective in deceiving the ordinary observer. The more conventional and immature hands that approximate a given system cause considerable difficulty in the test.

Calculating the percentage of actual identifications, on the basis of the possible number, for the groups of older and younger subjects respectively (twelve each), we find it 34 per cent. for the older group and 18.3 per cent. for the younger. The three reagents who completely failed to disguise their hands all belong to the older groups. Dropping these out and recalculating on the basis of actual to possible identifications we find the percentage of successful identification for the older group is 17.4 and for the younger 18.3 per cent.

Calculating the percentage in the same way, but with a division on the sex basis (twelve each), we find the percentage of correct identification is 22.5 in the case of the women and 30 per cent for the men. Again dropping out the three subjects who failed so signally at disguise (two women and one man) and recalculating, the percentages run 10.3 per cent for women and 24.7 per cent for the men. Our numbers are too small and too greatly affected by individual records to be of great value but so far as they go they indicate that women are more successful in disguise than men, and the younger penmen more successful than the older. All of the four subjects whose disguises were not penetrated were women (one from the older group, three from the younger). Of the eight specimens recognized by only one of the judges, four were written by men (three of the older, one of the younger group) and four by women (three of the younger group, one of the older). The best records, so far as disguises are concerned, are made by the young women.

The success of the younger group, particularly those writing an immature hand, is not necessarily due to the assumption of another graphic individuality. A return to the conventional system would cause a confusion of such a specimen with others similarly motivated. In a personal letter in which he comments upon the specimens used in the present test, Mr. Osborn writes me: "Writing by those who have not long been doing writing outside of school is bound to be simliar in many ways and when such writing is disguised its individual features may be modified and its general features remain, which would tend to connect specimens written by different writers." Yet this is not the whole story. In a few disguised specimens there is, very evidently, the assumption of a distinct, yet different individuality. The most interesting disguises are those in which there occur such curious changes in style. Some of these disguises come from the older group and lead to the conclusion that an effective disguise is much more a matter of the individual constitution than of age or even sex.

It has been held that ability to shift handwriting individuality is akin to ability in acting. But we have as yet no analysis of what traits characterize the dramatic type, although Holt suggsts (**25:35**) that "The actor's is merely the excessively mercurial and labile character." From my knowledge of my subjects I should say that those showing much facility in the adoption of another chirographic individuality, were, in the main, much more adaptable, more pliable, than the others. There is, however, one rather striking exception to this statement. This reagent—a girl of the younger group—is very visual in type and talented in drawing and fine handicraft. She took pleasure in producing for me an amazing variety of hands. Personally, she is of a distinct and somewhat inflexible individuality who yields slowly to social pressure. She is artistic, rather than imaginative.

Four of the subjects in this test were also reagents in my experiments on control processes in handwriting (R, B, S and D) (**14a**). For these I have a fairly complete analysis of their general procedure in writing. Of the four, two (R and B) were highly successful in their disguises and two (S and D) were inapt. D was particularly poor and that in spite of the fact that she was probably more aware than any other person who attempted the disguise, of the tell-tale points in chirography.

It is certainly significant that the alignment of these subjects in the test on handwriting disguise tallies with that found in the earlier experiment. R and B belong to the so-called "motor" group; D and S to the "sensory." Characteristic of the first group was the high degree to which writing was turned over to automatic control; characteristic of the second was the maintenance of conscious writing control, usually accompanied by a vivid sense of kinesthetic sensation. For the latter there is consciousness of muscular effort in writing and evidence of motor inhibition. For the first two the act of writing is successfully organized and the motor impulse smooth and effective. (**14a:14o f.**)

Interpreted on a conventional habit-basis one might perhaps expect the first two subjects to be less expert than the other two in disguise of the hand. But undoubtedly our conventional views of habit need reconstruction, especially along the line of ease in habit-breaking and the relation of this to the mental organization and constitution as a whole. Very possibly the cue to the interpretation must be sought in the smoothness, effectiveness, and lack of conflict in the motor impulses themselves, which would facilitate both habit-formation and quick readjustments.

A dramatic reaction to the instruction to disguise one's hand, in which one initiates and then yields confidently to a graphic-motor pattern somewhat different from his habitual one, is more effective in disguise than is an effortful disintegration of graphic details, with a constant effort at inhibition of habit. That both kinds of disguise may be successfully achieved, is, however, evident. Psychologically and practically they are of differing interest. The effortful disguise, although it may conceal its source effectively, will give evidence of not being a natural hand by inconsistencies, by retouching, and by the presence of fantastic forms. This type of disguise is, possibly, that most often found in the anonymous letter. The dramatic disguise will be less evidently a disguise and in its most successful forms points to an interesting mental type. It occurs in certain forms of forgery.

Meanwhile we note that Klages cites versatility in the shift of hands as characteristic of the fluidic personality. Indeterminate personalities have less to control or conquer. Graphic virtuosity is evidence of histrionic ability or of the split personality of the hysteric. The subject is worth investigation both in connection with a study of one type of criminal—the forger—and investigation of the hysteric temperament and of the double personality. Several possibilities of application suggest themselves in connection with the utilization of writing in diagnostic tests.

CHAPTER VI.

INTRA-INDIVIDUAL VARIABILITY.

In the preceding discussions we have had frequent occasion to emphasize individual variability in writing. The following study seeks to investigate the range of such variation in the writing of two subjects (I and II) and, in particular, to correlate variations in alignment, slant, and size with changes in emotional conditions.

The material was gathered in the following manner: For four months (October-February, 1913-14), in connection with another piece of experimental work, my collaborator and myself kept a daily handwriting record under standard conditions. At approximately the same hour of the day, usually at the same laboratory desk and with a pen of standard number, on a sheet of a given size and quality we (1) recorded the name, date, and pulse-rate; (2) wrote a paragraph on weather conditions; (3) gave a description of our physical condition; (4) recorded in detail our mood; and (5) summarized our interests for the day, rating the strength of each on an arbitrary numerical scale.

Our general problem was the gathering of material for a study of fluctuation in interests and in general patterns of consciousness. But I wished also to secure a standard series of writing specimens for analysis of graphic changes correlated with variability in condition. At the time, however, I had in mind no definite questions with reference to the particular points to be studied in connection with emotional variability, a condition which enhances the value of the material for the present purpose.

The series afford excellent stuff for such a study as I now wish to make, for the mood records of both subjects show considerable variation. There are, however, different factors concerned in the two.

For Subject I, the period under study proved to be one of very great emotional stress and strain, highly depressing in nature. On two occasions there occurred objective shocks of considerable intensity. Subjective fluctuations were also recorded. Periods of great absorption and interest in work were described and some of restless excitement but gay or happy moods were rather infrequent and in intensity were not comparable to the contrasting moods. The physical condition was poor, inducing rapid pulse, nervous irritability. and motor incoordination.

For Subject II, the mood changes were largely conditioned by varying physical conditions. The usual condition was one of energy and high interest in work, with occasional fatigue and lapse of interest in things in general. Three periods of low physical vitality were recorded, one incident to an attack of la grippe, the second an outcome of vaccination, the third the effect of an accident. A characteristic report of Subject II was the more or less periodic appearance of a day-dreaming mood, subjective in tone, pleasant, and accompanied by relaxation. A vacation period of ten days was toned by a sentimental and highly pleasurable mood.

My general procedure in checking over records was as follows: Under the appropriate date I listed the description of the physical condition and of the mood; I also listed the pulse and energy record, although I found these less complete than I would wish. I measured in millimeters and entered in my tabular summary the horizontal extension of each autograph, the height of three capitals in the name, the height or length of one three-space letter, and the slant of these same four letters. There are ninety autographs available for Subject I and one hundred and two for Subject II. The specific ways in which this tabulation was utilized will become apparent as the report develops.

Alignment was estimated in the following way: I measured with care the departure from the horizontal for the particular line on each sheet which recorded the mood, choosing this line because if content influences alignment, as graphologists report, it should most typically represent the condition for the day. This line was written about midway of the sheet—another reason for choosing it as representative. All the record sheets were of the same size (21.5 x 13.9 cm.) but on account of variability in marginal spacing there are some slight differences in line lengths. After measuring the departure from the horizontal of the line in question a general estimate of the tendency throughout the whole record was obtained. The measurements throughout are somewhat crude but probably sufficiently accurate for the purpose in hand. A more accurate measurement of writing amplitude by means of the curvimesser is in progress.

According to graphological tradition, alignment is determined to a large extent either by general temperamental tone or by the mood dominant at the moment of writing. The straight line characterizes the person of equable disposition; the up-tendency appears in the writing of enterprising, hopeful, optimistic penmen; and down-alignment in the productions of those of generally pessimistic inclination or of temporary depression, physical or mental. Cases are cited in the literature in which great variations in alignment result from shift in mood. Slant is also cited as dependent upon emotional instability. Size, so far as related to mood, would show increased amplitude in energetic, hopeful states and decrease in size in depressive states.

To determine whether the mental condition had any effect upon these three graphic elements, I checked over my tabulation of moods and selected, *wholly at random*, six for each subject, under the three following descriptions:

I. No emotional toning to consciousness. Neutral.

II. Consciousness toned with gayety, happiness.

III. Consciousness toned with depression, melancholy, or physical sickness.

Only five entries under the second rubric were discoverable for Subject I.

TABLE II Subject I

Date	Mood	Physical Condition	Energy	Horizontal Extension	Height	Slant	Alignment
I NEUTRAL. OBJECTIVE-MINDED.							
Oct. 18	Work-mood	Excellent	+	75	49	25.6	Up 2. Gen. tendency up.
Nov. 8	Objective	Tired	?	63	36	42.0	Up 2. Gen. tendency up.
Nov. 28	Objective	Fair	+	44	45	22.0	Convex. Gen. tendency straight.
Nov. 29	Objective	Fair	++	83	40	35.0	Up 4. Gen. tendency up.
Dec. 1	Alert	Good	++	55	30	30.6	Up 5. Gen. tendency up.
Jan. 5	Objective	Good	?	54	33	26.0	Up 5. Gen. tendency up.
			(Av.)	62.3	38.8	30.2	
II CONSCIOUSNESS TONED WITH GAYETY, HAPPINESS. (Not comparable in Intensity to moods of depression)							
Nov. 3	Pleased	Good	?	60	38	31	Convex. Gen. tendency convex.
Nov. 6	Happy	Good	?	51	32	31	Up 2. Gen. tendency up.
Dec. 3	Gay	Good	+	62	40	33	Up 9. Gen. tendency up.
Dec. 4	Contented	Fair	?	66	45	21.6	Up 4. Gen. tendency up.
Dec. 19	Gay	Good	+	65	38	28	Up 4. Gen. tendency up.
			(Av.)	60.8	38.6	28.9	
III CONSCIOUSNESS TONED BY DEPRESSION.							
Oct. 14	Sad	Bad+	—	46	39	16	Up 4. Gen. tendency straight. (Bad shock)
Oct. 16	Frightened Worried	Headache	—	60	42	31	Down 2. Gen. tendency variable. Emotionally exhausted.
Oct. 30	Depression	Fair	?	68	44	26	Up 6. Gen. tendency up.
Nov. 17	Depression	Bad	—	65	42	22	Concave. Gen. tendency concave.
Nov. 21	Futility-feeling	Bad	?	55	38	35	Up 4. Gen. tendency up.
Dec. 20	Depression	Collapse	—	52	30	23	Down 2. Gen. tendency down. (Physical exhaustion)
			(Av.)	57.6	39.1	25.5	

TABLE III Subject II

Date	Mood	Physical Condition	Energy	Horizontal Extension	Height	Slant	Alignment
I NEUTRAL							
Oct. 7	Wide-awake	Nervous	++	110	37	41.6	Up 2. Gen. tendency up.
Nov. 6	Keen for Work	Well	++	84	28	26.0	Down 4. Gen. tendency down.
Dec. 5	Plugging	Fair	+	59	24	27.6	Down 4. Gen. tendency variable.
Jan. 2	Business-like	Good	++	80	28	11.0	Down 3.
Jan. 8	Neutral	Good	+	70	27	7.6	Straight, Gen. tendency variable.
Jan. 13	Everyday	Poor	+	66	16	4.6	Down 5. Gen. tendency variable.
			(Av.)	78	28.3	19.7	
II CONSCIOUSNESS PLEASURABLY TONED							
Oct. 16	Happy	Well	+	93	33	19.0	Down 3. Gen. tendency down.
Oct. 31	Enthusiastic	Well	++	84	28	29.0	Convex Gen. tendency up.
Nov. 15	Happy; lazy	Fair	—	67	29	35.6	Up 3. Gen. tendency up.
Nov. 29	Pleased	Fair	++	95	22	46.6	Up 2. Gen. tendency up.
Dec. 26	Sentimental	?	—	92	57	43.0	Up 3. Gen. tendency up.
Jan. 7	Gay	Good	++	104	45	52.6	Very irregular.
			(Av.)	86	35.6	37.6	
III CONSCOUSNESS TONED BY DEPRESSION OR SICKNESS.							
Oct. 29	Doubting	Tired	—	89	37	45.6	Concave Gen. tendency variable.
Nov. 7	Depressed	Fair	++	61	22	34.0	Down 3 Gen. tendency down.
Nov. 10	Despondent	Fair	—	68	29	34.0	Straight Gen. tendency variable.
Nov. 14	Displeased	Tired	—	98	31	46.6	Fall at one point.
Nov. 27	Depressed	Sick	—	53	18	16.0	Down 3 Gen. tendency variable.
Dec. 13	Self-Disgust	Good	?	56	20	23.6	Up 3 Gen. tendency up.
			(Av.)	70.8	26	33.8	

Tables II and III summarize the results. Size and slant measurements were made on the autograph as explained above. Under extension, the horizontal extension of the whole name is entered; under height the *SUM* in millimeters of the measurements on the four chosen letters; under slant the average degree of slant from the vertical for the chosen letters.

Some interesting facts emerge from study of the individual records. First, that of great variability in all the elements measured. Thus for Subject I, length of name ranges from forty-four to eighty-three millimeters; extension of the first initial from ten to twenty-nine millimeters; average slant on the chosen letters from sixteen to forty-two degrees. For Subject II, the length of name ranges from fifty-three to one hundred and ten millimeters, extension of the initial capital from five to twenty-six millimeters; and average slant from less than five to nearly fifty-three degrees. Both penmen show, I suspect, an unusually extensive range of variation for the traits measured. Both show on occasion a tendency toward excessive slant; toward the left for I; toward the right for II.

The tabulation of the specific records indicates that results from Subject II offer some confirmation of graphological principles. Average extension, height and slant are all increased in a pleasurable state whether comparison is instituted with the products of the neutral state or with those of depressed conditions. Not only is this true, but, furthermore, depressive states also show, in conjunction with decrease in amplitude, an increase in slant as compared with the neutral, quite in accordance with graphological expectation. Alignment presents less straightforward results. In general, Subject II produces a very irregular alignment. One can assert this much only, that there is a trifle greater tendency to up-alignment when consciousness is pleasurably toned than is the case otherwise.

Results from Subject I are very different. In this instance the records produced in the neutral or objective-minded states exceed the others in extension and slant; there is very little difference in result between depressive and gay states. Alignment which is normally rising shows a considerable inclination to fall in depression.

There was undoubtedly some difference in the significance of the so-called neutral state for the two subjects. For I, the real contrast between the first and the other two conditions is expressed by the terms Objective-Subjective (possibly extroverted-introverted). The objective state of mind is characterized by intense interest and absorption in work; it is unemotional but probably pleasant and is more characterized by energy than the contrasting states are. For Subject II, the opposition is between indifferent and affectively toned states of mind. States of great interest in work and of physical energy are happy states. Depression is, usually, the outcome of sickness. For both subjects, however, a relationship exists between energy and the resulting graphic expression. With high energy there is, in general, an increase in scope of movement.

Anticipating a distinction to be emphasized later, we may say that Subject II writes a typically explosive hand,—large, light, rapid, centrifugal, tied together, with excess of occasional movements and little distinction in proportions. Subject I writes an inhibited hand, small, somewhat slow, centripetal and broken, with great distinction in relative proportions. Alignment is the contradictory symptom in each of these hands, since I shows a tendency to rising alignment and II a tendency to falling alignment. Release of tension such as occurs in states of unself-conscious absorption in work shows in I's case in the production of a hand more explosive than usual, increased in amplitude, speed, and continuity. Attention is diverted from the graphic product. II, naturally of a more objective mental set, exhibits under pleasurable excitement increasing impulse but under depression, restraint of movement.

While such results are of very great interest they suggest from the practical side the difficulty inherent in any at-

TABLE IV

Subject I					Subject II				
Horizontal Extension	Slant	Energy	Physical Condition	Mood	Horizontal Extension	Slant	Energy	Physical Condition	Mood
83	35	++	Fair	Absorbed in Work	110	41.6	++	Wide awake	Neutral
75	34	—	Fair	Indifferent	110	31.0	?	Good?	Sentimental
75	25.6	—	Excellent	Work-mood	109	44	?	Sleepy	Sluggish
72	28	+	Good	Objective	105	46	—	?	Neutral
70	26	?	Poor	Depressed	104	32	?	Good?	Sentimental
69	33	?	Fair	Objective	I04	45	?	Good	Gay
69	34	?	Bad	Indifferent	102	30	?	Good?	Humorous
68	26	?	Fair	Depressed	100	39	—	Good	Dreamy
67	32	—	Poor	Indifferent	100	45	++	Good	Pleased
67	42	?	Poor	Depressed	98	41	?	Good?	Sentimental
43	19	—	Well	Indifferent	53	18	—	Grippe	Depressed
44	31	?	Fair	Indifferent	56	26	—	Sleepy	Quiescent
44	22	+	Fair	Work-mood	57	36	+	Poor	Optimistic
44	25	?	Fair	Over-worked	56	23	?	Good	Self-disgust
46	16	—	Bad	Shocked	58	27	+	Fair	Energetic
46	22	?	Good	Pleasant-unpleasant	58	21	+	Tired	Work-mood
47	19	+	Well+	Emotional	59	12	—	Tired	Neutral
47	20	—	Sleepy	Discouraged	59	25	—	Tired	Passive
50	30	—	Bad	Indifferent	59	27.6	?	Fair	Work-mood
50	29	?	Good	Common-sense	59	17	—	Fair	Dreamy

tempt at utilizing size and slant apart from an understanding of the particular case involved; only under prescribed conditions can increase and decrease of size and slant be revelatory. Fluctuations in alignment offer still greater difficulties in interpretation.

As a second method of testing the records, I selected material for tabulation, starting not from the mood-side but from the measurements I had listed under extension. I took the highest and lowest ten per cent. of these measurements. Table IV. gives the tabulation with correlative data.

This tabulation reveals little more than the earlier ones. As before, a greater agreement with graphological principles is manifest in the record of Subject II than in that of Subject I. But the records of both subjects show numerous exceptions to the general point of view. When energy is high and there is an active, working, happy mood, there is a tendency for Subject II to produce magnified writing but the same tendency is evident in nervous cross moods, and in the relaxed condition incident to day-dreaming. Subject I also, when nervously "on edge," indulges in excess movement. It appears from the figures that increased slant and increased horizontal extension are pretty closely associated, an association which one might anticipate on mechanical grounds since the degree of inclination of the connecting stroke would greatly influence the extent of territory covered by the graphic product. A question suggests itself as to the possibility of untangling this mechanical relationship in graphological interpretation! Just at present, however, we are not called upon to attempt such a feat. The record of Subject II affords, however, some interesting examples of slant and extension in mechanical opposition, since under depression writing may be at once more compact and more centrifugal than is usually the case.

If we turn to extreme individual records we find several observations worthy of note. Thus the extreme up-alignment for Subject II, a rise of eight millimeters, is recorded on November 8, just preceding a football game in which II was intensely interested. The mood was characterized as one of strain and excitement, certainly hyperkinetic, but not describable as pleasurable or the reverse. On November 20, when the subject was ill with la grippe, the writing shows a falling alignment, varying from two to thirteen millimeters. The maximal slant (nearly fifty-three degrees) occurs for Subject II on two days when the subject was in a humorous mood, incident to editing the "yellow" number of the college paper.

It is noticeable that often a given mood prevailed for a number of days and continued to color graphic expression. Thus, a number of II's extreme records fall in one and the same week, a vacation period toned with a pleasant sentimental mood that magnified and inclined his writing. Four of the contrasting records occur in one week and in the week following five others; during this interval the subject was struggling with la grippe.

A number of Subject I's most diminutive specimens are found in the first week of the experiment. The explanation is obvious. There was definite concentration upon the graphic product which resulted, as we have reason to expect, in small, even, somewhat vertical writing.

On the whole, the results of the experiment were most enlightening. An increase in graphic movement accompanies heightened energy, while changes in slant and alignment appear influenced by emotional conditions but not in in unequivocal way.

CHAPTER VII.

GRAPHIC INDIVIDUALITY.

The assertion is frequently made that graphic individuality is but a specific example of a pattern that is impressed upon all the expressive movements of a given person. How may one prove or disprove such an assertion? Obviously not by casual observations which are subject to two very serious sources of error: (1) the difficulty of accurately reporting on the individual character of expressive or graphic patterns and (2) the biassing of observation in both cases by a definite mental attitude which predisposes one to see similarity or difference between the two.

As a control on such comparison it seems necessary that the observations on the graphic and expressive pattern should be made by different persons. It would be well if each judge were ignorant of the specific point at issue, namely, the extent to which the two sets of judgments would be found to agree or disagree. In the simple test about to be reported, this ignorance of the purpose of the experiment existed only in the case of the observers of the expressive movements. I myself passed judgment on the handwriting pattern.

My first attempt at handling the situation was unsuccessful. After careful study of the handwriting of fourteen students in one of my classes I attempted to describe the graphic individuality of each by five carefully chosen descriptive adjectives. From these adjectives I prepared a list of words which I gave to the class, requesting each member to choose three which should characterize as accurately as possible the carriage, walk, and manner of gesture of each member of the class. A comparison of these latter judgments with those I had passed on handwriting showed cases of both agreement and disagreement.

I had, for example, characterized P's hand as expert, graceful, mincing, rapid, and self-conscious. The following tabulation was made of the judgments on his expressive movements: Neat, 7; graceful, 3; mincing, 3; expert (including fluent), 5; energetic, 2; conventional, 2; easy, 2; diminutive, 1; decided, 1; affected, 1; smooth, 2; finished, 2; matter-of-fact, 2. The most frequently chosen adjective is "neat" which might have been applied to P's writing with great appropriateness. As his writing is small, "diminutive" might also have been applied, etc. But, obviously, the adjectives chosen were not sufficiently distinctive.

In at least one case, a very evident disagreement between handwriting and type of movement is recorded. The observers agree fairly well on Pt. Her manner and walk are characterized as decided, energetic, matter-of-fact, and rapid. Her writing was characterized as neat, unaggressive, unemphatic, and diminutive.

On the whole, however, the test proved of little value, not only because of the vagueness of adjectives selected, but also because of the inconclusiveness of the judgments passed on the expressive movements. There are instances in which twenty-one out of a possible thirty-four adjectives were applied to one and the same person.

Accordingly I planned a new experiment. In order to control observations more definitely I decided to submit contrasting adjectives, with instructions to apply one of each pair to the individual whose walk, carriage, and manner of gesturing were under observation. Furthermore, I adopted as a general principle for choice of adjectives the distinctions that seem to hold for the contrasting types of explosive and inhibited writing. This resulted in a series of paired adjectives as follows: Rapid or slow; light or heavy; loose or compact; expansive or restrained; adroit or maladroit; fluent or jerky (tense); angular or supple (rounded); conventional or individual; impulsive or deliberate; concentric or eccentric.

A blank record was prepared consisting of these paired adjectives under the instructions, "Please study the walk, carriage, and gestures of the persons who are listed below and then classify their usual movements under *one* of *each* of the following terms." The list of names given was carefully selected and limited to twelve, as the passing of a real judgment demands considerable effort of attention. With this in mind I also selected my collaborators with care. Six student judges were utilized, five of whom carried out the exercise as part of their experimental work on the general topic of expressive movement, in connection with other experiments under the same general heading. Their work was done very conscientiously. In addition, I asked five faculty colleagues to pass judgment, selecting each for some definite reason; one, for example, was instructor in dramatics.

My collaborators reported great difficulty in passing these judgments. Most of them observed for some weeks the individuals listed before they recorded their impressions. The classification "concentric-eccentric" seemed particularly difficult to handle, possibly because the concept was a somewhat novel one. A note had, however, been appended to the question blank, defining concentric as movement toward the body as a center; eccentric as movement away from the body. "Notice, for example, whether the elbows are carried in or out, etc." Next to this division, that of "conventional-individual" was found most difficult to manage. The terms "adroit" and "maladroit" proved ambiguous; either grace or skill or expertness might be emphasized. In some instances judges found themselves utterly unable to reach a decision on some particular point for some particular person observed, so that there are inequalities in the number of judgments returned. Only seven judges returned records for P—not because of any particular difficulty in handling his case, but because of lack of acquaintance with him and failure in opportunity to study his form of expression.

Before giving out my blanks for these records, my judgments on the handwriting had been filed away. In some cases I found great difficulty in reaching a decision and at many points dissatisfaction with my record. I tried very conscientiously to dismiss from my thoughts any characteristics of an individual other than his handwriting, but it would be impossible to assert that I succeeded absolutely in such an endeavor. The rubrics which caused me the greatest trouble were "Light-Heavy" and "Individual-Conventional." Note 1. I had little confidence in either of these sets of judgments except in a few extreme instances. My judgment on the division "Fluent or Jerky (tense)" was influenced by a study of the line-quality under the microscope. My observation on "Rapid-Slow" was based on general appearance. But it was possible to obtain, later, timed records from all my subjects and to compare these records with an order of merit arrangement earlier made by myself. The correlational coefficient was .55 when the arrangement was based on the normal writing and .61 when the correlation was made with speeded writing. My biggest errors in judgment was underrating the speed of D3's hand and overestimating that of P—errors which were not confirmed by my collaborators' judgments on expression.

In passing judgment on concentric or eccentric movement I gave attention to slant. I grouped three specimens under the rubrics "concentric"; one was a backhand (L); a second (S1) presented numerous examples of what the French call "écriture sinistrogyre," that is, curves or terminal strokes turned in the reversed direction. S2 approached a vertical hand. D3 was classed as "eccentric" but after considerable hesitation; this hand will, I believe, become later a backhand, although as yet it follows the conventional slant. D3 has since, in fact, informed me that in very rapid and careless writing there is a strong tendency to slant toward the left.

[Note 1. I do not feel at all confident just what pair of terms should be utilized in discriminating between the explosive and the inhibited hand with reference to this point. In the present set of judgments I interpreted "individual" as equivalent to "easily identified," but such a definition causes an inclusion in such category of hands that are stylistic (S1) as well as those that are original. A stylistic hand is, probably, inhibited. On the other hand, a careless hand (W1), as such, shows explosive tendencies but it may not depart very far from a conventional style.]

Table V gives a detailed survey of the results. The judgments on the expressive movements are summed under the appropriate heads while in the third column of each set the graphological judgment is indicated by the initial letter of the chosen term. A question mark after this initial indicates uncertainty in decision; a plus mark shows that the quality was evident to a high degree; a minus sign indicates the reverse.

As a rough approximation of the agreement between the two sets of judgments we may take the percentage of cases in which the graphological judgment is in agreement with the expressive judgment. Chance would account for a fifty per cent agreement; the actual agreement is 60.5 per cent, enough higher than chance to point an interesting problem. But such summary disposal of records is of much less interest than detailed perusal. For example, there are individuals whose expressive movements are obviously characterized with ease as shown by the preponderance of judgments in one direction or another; there are others whose movements are most difficult to classify. As example of the first type we have A1, D1, D2, P, S1; of the second, D3, H, L, W. Agreement of the expressive with the graphic judgment is fairly consistent for A2, D1, H, P, S1; less evident for B1, D2, S2, and W; for A1 and D3 there is noteworthy disagreement between the two sets of judgment; the judgments on L are balanced. Agreement in the two sets of judgments is, on the whole, more pronounced in case of the men, (A2, D1, B, S1, S2, and P) than of the women, (A1, D2, D3, H, L, and W). H is an outstanding exception to this statement. A greater degree of conventionality in either expression or handwriting on the part of women probably explains this result.

TABLE V

Expressive and Graphic Movements

	Rapid	Slow	Writing	Light	Heavy	Writing	Loose	Compact	Writing	Expansive	Restrained	Writing	Adroit	Maladroit	Writing	Fluent	Jerky	Writing	Angular	Rounded	Writing	Conventional	Individual	Writing	Impulsive	Deliberate	Writing	Concentric	Eccentric	Writing	Agreement	No decision	Disagreement
A1	1	10	S	2	9	L	7	4	C	3	8	E?	5	6	A	8	2	F	7	3	R	4	5	C	1	10	D	8	3	E	3	0	7
A2	7	4	R	3	8	H	9	2	C	7	4	R	1	7	M+	1	9	J	10	1	A	4	7	C	6	5	I ?	3	8	E	7	0	3
B1	1	11	R+	5	6	L?	5	5	L	11	0	E	8	2	A	9	2	J	2	9	R	3	8	I	5	6	I+	2	8	E+	5	1	4
D1	10	1	R+	8	3	L	10	1	C	8	3	R	2	9	A?	1	10	J+	10	1	A	3	7	I+	6	5	I	2	8	E	7	0	3
D2	11	0	R	11	0	H?	0	10	L	7	4	E	9	2	M?	9	1	F	0	11	R	5	5	C	9	2	I	3	7	E—	6	1	3
D3	10	0	S	8	2	H	7	2	L?	8	2	R	6	3	M	7	3	J	6	4	A	4	5	C	10	0	D	3	7	E?	3	0	7
H1	9	2	R	5	6	H+	6	5	L	6	5	E	4	6	M	2	10	F	10	1	A	4	7	I	6	5	I	4	7	E—	9	0	1
L1	7	2	S	5	5	L	4	6	C	4	6	R	7	2	M+	5	4	F	2	8	A	7	3	C?	7	3	D	5	5	C	4	2	4
P1	4	3	R	7	0	L	1	6	L?	1	6	E	6	0	A+	5	2	F	0	7	R	6	1	C+	0	7	I	5	2	E+	6	0	4
S1	1	10	S	6	5	L	1	10	C	1	10	R	9	1	A	8	1	F	2	9	R	7	3	I	0	11	D	5	6	C	8	0	2
S2	0	9	S	1	9	L?	2	6	L?	1	8	R	2	6	M	4	4	J	3	6	A	8	1	C	0	9	D	6	3	C?	6	1	3
W1	10	1	R	8	3	H?	6	5	L	10	1	E?	7	4	M	5	6	F?	5	5	A?	1	10	C	11	0	I	2	9	E	5	1	4
Agreement Expressive and graphic judgment			9			5			5			7			6			7			8			6			8			8	69		
No decision			0			1			1			0			0			1			1			1			0			1		6	
Disagreement			3			6			6			5			6			4			3			5			4			3			45

Age, even more than sex, cuts expressive tendencies. The younger members of the group as such exhibit more impulsive and free movement than the older members. For D3 and L youth masks inhibitory tendencies very evident in their handwriting. But on the graphic side the effects are reversed; age, with increasing graphic expertness, may lend an impetuosity to handwriting movements which walk and gesture lack. The record of B (one of the older group) should be studied in this connection. B's writing is impetuous and excessively rapid in appearance. By the timed records on normal writing it ranks second of the twelve. Note 2. But the general effect of carriage and walk is slow and deliberate, although B's gestures are quick and impulsive. There is only one dissenting judgment in rating him as slow in movement; that dissenting record is given by the instructor in dramatics who has had frequent occasion to study B's movements in amateur theatricals.

Next to age, the confusion of certain bodily characteristics with movement seems to me a frequent source of conflict in classification. Thus B is heavy of body but rather extraordinarily light of movement if one discriminate with care; D3, on the contrary, is excessively slight in build but relatively heavy of step. The situation is further complicated by the tendency to allow supposed mental traits to influence the judgment on expression. One subject for observation exhibits considerable inertia in getting down to work but after beginning proceeds with great celerity and with quick decision. This trait of inertia introduced difficulty in classification of him as impulsive or deliberate.

If we turn from the individuals who were observed to the rubrics employed we find that there is greatest agreement in the two sets of judgments under the headings Rapid-Slow; Angular-Rounded; Impulsive-Deliberate; and Concentric-Eccentric. Agreement is less pronounced on Expansive-Restrained; Fluent-Jerky; and Conventional-Individual.

[Note 2. In the speeded records B ties for first place. If speed were accurately calculated on the basis of time per millimeter, he would undoubtedly rank first by a safe margin, as his writing is very large. B's speed could be increased by a reduction in size of letters, a device which would certainly be adopted by a penman of different mental type.]

There is slight preponderance in disagreement for the rubrics, Light-Heavy and Loose-Compact and only chance distribution for Adroit-Maladroit. Some disagreement is probably to be attributed to ambiguity in the terms themselves. Thus I found myself interpreting "adroit" as equivalent to "expert," "skillful," while I am inclined to think that my collaborators stressed "grace." The records on concentric expression deserve particular study as the results are most suggestive, and the agreement more extensive than appears in a crude summing up by totals. Only in the case of P is there striking disagreement. As my judgments had in this case a rather definitely determined objective basis, the results are enhanced in value.

In conclusion, it may be stated that the outcome of the experiment is slightly in favor of an agreement between graphic and expressive movement but that the whole trend of the results is indicative of the great difficulty inherent in observation of expressive movement and the absence of all standards for reference. Certainly no sweeping assertion of general similarity can be ventured, although for a few traits there is strong evidence of such harmony. It is rather interesting to note in this connection that the percentage of successes when judgments on character (see chap. VIII) were related to particular graphic traits was usually higher than that reported here. In the character investigation, I had, however, the assistance of much more expert collaborators than in the experiments on graphic individuality.

CHAPTER VIII.

GRAPHOLOGICAL STUDY OF THE HAND-WRITING OF PSYCHOLOGISTS.

In 1906, Binet published his most interesting treatise on "Les révélations de l'écriture d'après un contrôle scientifique," wherein he presented the results of a series of carefully controlled tests designed to answer the following questions: Does handwriting reveal sex, age, degree of intelligence, character?

We have already had occasion to refer to Binet's conclusions with reference to revelation by handwriting of age and sex. Here we may briefly summarize his conclusions as to determination of intelligence and character from handwriting. Binet concludes that intelligence is revealed in chirography although the extent of this revelation varies with the individual; the graphic signs of intelligence, granted an incontestable reality, are not always found in the writing of a man of great intelligence. In selecting from paired specimens the hands produced by the more intelligent of the penmen, Crépieux-Jamin gave 91 per cent. of successes. (**3c:101**.) But the graphological portraits, correct so far as they go, are often extremely vague. It is this vagueness that needs to be cleared up by greater precision in definition and interpretation of graphological signs. Perhaps the conservative statement that there is more truth than error in the judgments of graphologists anent intelligence sums up Binet's records on this point. Concerning his tests on the revelation of character in writing we may cite the general conclusion that the errors in reading character from writing are much greater than those found in reading intelligence and that the graphologists show greater uncertainty in the second than in the first test. In actual figures, Crépieux-Jamin's percentage of successes was but 73 as compared with 91 for intelligence (**3c:248**), where a chance success of 50 might have been anticipated.

Binet's interest in the above investigations centered largely in discovering a method for testing graphological conclusions. The question of method is, in fact, crucial. In the experiment I wish to report here I have endeavored to check up a chosen number of graphological principles by utilizing a modified form of the order of merit method. In many respects my procedure was very different from that of Binet. In the first place I was obliged to dispense with the services of professional graphologists. In lieu of their interpretations I had recourse to measurements and observations on certain graphic signs that could be made by myself and which could serve as a basis for a serial arrangement. This arrangement I shall refer to briefly as the graphological arrangement. To obtain a characterological arrangement for correlation with the graphological one I was obliged to ask help from a number of psychologists whose average judgment on a given individual I have taken as my basis for comparison.

I may describe my procedure under four heads: (1) choice of graphic elements for measurement; (2) determination of graphological scheme; (3) material to be used in the experiment; (4) questionary and collaborators.

(1) For graphic traits I was anxious to utilize as far as it was possible the same elements that I had studied in preceding sections of this book, namely size, slant, alignment, continuity, line-quality or pressure, and proportion. These graphic elements lent themselves in a greater or less degree to objective measurement, so that it was possible on the basis of such measurements to arrange a given collection of hands into groups which represented a graded series in which a given external character was present to a greater or less extent. As a matter of fact with reference to actual details the procedure was not quite as simple as the above statement would suggest. Modifications will become apparent in the specific discussions that follow.

(2) Difficulties enough presented themselves when I tried to correlate some simple graphological scheme with each

of the above mentioned elements. As finally worked out I attempted a test of each of the following assumptions: I. Small or filiform writing as an evidence of interest in minutiae or details in preference to preoccupation with principles; II. Large writing and, in particular, large capitals in comparison with one-space letters as an indication of pride, hopefulness; III. Degree of discontinuity or disconnectedness of script as symptomatic of speculative or inductive type of intellect in contrast to deductive or assimilative type of thinking; IV. Pressure or line-quality and peculiar forms of stroke as significant of aggressiveness; V. Variation in slant and alignment as symptomatic of temperament; VI. A complex of traits as symptomatic of an explosive versus an inhibited make-up.

(3) The collection utilized was a series of letters from thirty-six psychologists, most of whom were fairly well known. There are both advantages and disadvantages inherent in the choice of a closely selected group of individuals. Such a close selection probably rules out extremes of difference such as one might expect to find in a more miscellaneous group and so decreases the index of correlation. But in testing the significance of a specific detail it seemed worth while keeping fairly constant such factors as general culture, general intelligence, and general character stability.

Several of my collaborators commented on the effect of utilizing such a group of subjects. One remarks, "Is it not to be expected that your list, which includes only those who have a certain measure of success in psychology, would fall in the medium class?"

And another wrote as follows: "In taking a group of well known psychologists you have a group of successful people —which means in general a group whose members do not differ outrageously from the social norm in social qualities and in energy and the qualities connected therewith deviate in the direction of excess. Indeed as psychologists and as successful they are a somewhat narrowly limited group." Such a description is well worth keeping in mind.

(4) My collaborators in this experiment, whose group judgment I utilized in getting a characterological rating, consisted of twelve well-known psychologists who had had considerable opportunity to know well many of the other psychologists whose writing I was utilizing in the test. To each of my collaborators I sent a list of thirty-six names with the request that each individual be classified under some one division of each of the given rubrics. The specific groups utilized were as follows:

Group I. Preoccupation with Details in Contrast with Interest in General Principles; Five Divisons.

1. Preoccupation with details.	2. Love of minutiae; critical, but wider interest than 1.	3. Balanced attention to details and principles. 4. Details	subordinated. Interest in far-reaching projects.	5. Details ignored. Speculative, poetic type.

Group II. Feeling of Self-Worth (Pride); Five Divisions.,

1. Strong Feeling of Self-Worth.	2. Moderated Feeling of Self-Worth.	3. Average Feeling of Self-Worth.	4. Modest estimate of self.	5. Excessive modesty.

Group III. Originality, Judgment and Assimilative Capacity: Four Divisions.

1. Original, Fertile-minded; little judgment or power of organization.	2. Original, fertile-minded plus power of judgment.	3. Logical type; combinative activity.	4. Assimilative capacity; utilization of ideas of others. Neither critical nor ingenious.

Group IV. Five Divisions on the Ground of Aggressiveness.

1. Very aggressive; enjoys fighting; dogmatic.	2. Strongly aggressive; positive but not unreasonable.	3. Mediumly aggressive.	4. Non-aggressive; avoids a fight.	5. Passive; suggestible; yielding.

Group V. Classification on Basis of Temperament; Five Divisions.

1. Optimistic; hopeful; enterprising.	2. Cheerful; active.	3. Equable; evenly active.	4. Moody, variable. Fluctuating attitude toward work.	5. Pessimistic philosophy.

Group VI. Explosive versus Inhibited Type of Activity; Five Division.

1. Excessive Impulsion.	2. Moderated Impulsion.	3. Balanced Impulsion.	4. Strong and uneven Inhibition.	5. Excessive Inhibition.

Before giving the results of the investigation I wish to call attention to a number of factors which undoubtedly operated to reduce a correlation that might have been obtained under more favorable conditions.

My utilization of the graphological material was, of course, somewhat mechanical. It is abundantly open to criticism. In the first place I do not possess the background that a professional graphologist would have and in the second place I made little effort to modify the outcome of mechanical measurement by what graphologists call the total complex. In fact, I deliberately avoided any attempt to utilize the graphological portrait as a whole and leaned rather heavily upon details, with the very definite purpose of testing as stringently as possible certain specific assumptions, with the assurance that positive results would thereby be enhanced in value. Such procedure also protected me from a possible inclination to be somewhat influenced by the professional reputation of the penmen. My personal acquaintance was limited to a few of the number. While on the whole I rested my case largely on a few specific measurements, there were times when I was obliged to have recourse to a balancing of two or more graphic signs. Under such circumstances my weighting of individual elements was necessarily arbitrary as I could obtain little assistance from the treatises on the subject.

Another prolific source of error was the possible multiplicity of causes for the same effect. Thus, increase in size of writing may be determined by decrease in illumination or increase in automatism or effort to mask a lack of motor control. I had, of course, no knowledge of the conditions under which the letters I was using had been produced and no specific information concerning the penmen. In several cases I should greatly like to know whether or not vision is normal. Occasionally an age factor is slightly evident.

Probably the most significant source of error in the present investigation was the lack in a number of instances of sufficient material to justify a judgment. In the case of two specimens I was certainly reckless in attempting to pass judgment. One specimen (2) consisted of two lines scrawled with great precipitancy at the close of a typed letter and the other (6) of a few words filling in the blanks on a printed card. I have omitted my measurements on these specimens from one or two groups as I shall specify later. Specimen 8 was also very meagre.

So far as letter-content was concerned, my collection was a fairly comparable one. Different size of letter sheets probably introduced some slight uncertainty in judgment on size but, on the whole, this source of error was negligible.

So much from the graphological side. A few words concerning the difficulties encountered by my collaborators in the characterological judgment. Apart from the difficulty inherent in breaking up such a closely selected group, there was the error arising from insufficient acquaintance with an individual or, at least, a more extensive acquaintance with some of the psychologists than with others. As an outcome of my returns I found it necessary to discard six of the names included in my original list because of failure to receive a sufficient number of judgments to justify obtaining an average. Moreover, I did not receive for every grouping complete returns even for the twenty-nine remaining names. My averages are obtained from individual items varying from seven to twelve in number. Apparently my collaborators found greatest difficulty in passing judgment on Temperament, and on the Explosive-Inhibited make-up.

It is, moreover, evident that the categories I adopted leave much to be desired in the way of logical classification. Such inadequacy was, in part at least, due to the difficulty I found in reducing graphological implications to any form of system. Rigid definition of rubrics might have been attempted, but I thought best in the present exploration to employ somewhat elastic terms.

The attempt to work out a serial arrangement of handwriting specimens is something of a strain upon even the most confident graphological principles. I have, therefore, tabulated for each specimen under each rubric the graphological group in which it was placed before the shaded arrangement was made and I have given in parallel columns the most common placement by my collaborators and the mean variation from this mode. When the same number of judgments was given for two adjacent groups, an intermediate point between the two is indicated. When such a distribution occurred for groups not adjacent, the mid-group was used only when the shading from one to the other was a quantitative one. Only a few cases of this sort appear. See Table VI.

From a study of this table a number of conclusions become evident which are not revealed by the citation of the correlational coefficients. Such a tabulation enables us, moreover, to pass from a mass treatment of results to an estimation of the individual successes or failures that might be anticipated from a graphological analysis. An individual, rather than statistical treatment, is, of course, the desideratum in diagnostic tests.

1. *Small or filiform writing as an evidence of interest in detail in contrast with speculative interests.*

The correlation of an unusually small and precise hand with love of minutiae and critical acumen, in contrast with interest in far-reaching projects and speculative principles, is a common one in the books on the subjects. Accordingly I decided to classify my collection of hands in five groups to correspond with the characterological divisions previously given: (1) Preoccupation with details; (2) Love of minutiae; critical, but wider interests than 1; (3) Balanced attention to details and principles; (4) Details subordinated; interest in far-reaching projects; (5) Details ignored; speculative; poetic.

In making my classification for this purpose I had recourse to actual measurement of size of letters. I was interested in absolute size, not in proportional size, for example the relative size of small and capital letters, a matter of concern in another study. While small and narrow writing indicates love of detail, we have other graphic characters that should be considered with it and these I utilized in getting my group classification as follows: Regularity and invariability of writing; even spacing of words and lines; clear and sufficient formation of letters; care for punctuation. An order of merit was prepared with these points in mind. The contrasting hand involved the presence of one or more of the following traits: Rounded strokes; extra loops and high placed i-dot; rising alignment; insufficiently clear letters and letters larger at the end than at the beginning of a word.

In using absolute size of writing as a basis of classification, one encounters the following difficulty, namely, that size is a most variable aspect of writing; it is influenced by many factors, such as size of paper, the pen one uses, illumination, physical condition, the care with which one writes. Moreover, the group from which my collection came was a closely selected one and did not show the range of variation in this respect that would be exhibited by a more miscellaneous collection. The miniscules ranged in height from less than .5 to 5 mm. My notes show the following observations: "Almost all of these hands show attention to detail in the clear-cut stroke and complete letter-form. There are few 'speculative' hands among them." And again, after completion of my arrangement, "I find it very difficult to make an order of merit. Many of the hands are both *large and clear-cut.* The final rating throws more emphasis on even, complete, and careful writing than on absolute size. Hands 7, 22, 9, 29 are taken as the central group because they show to a high degree signs of both critical acumen and interest in principles. The less evident cases are thrown into groups 2 and 4. Groups 1 and 5 present some interesting extremes. Except for groups 1 and 5, I have absolutely no confidence in this grouping."

But in spite of this lack of confidence the correlation between the graphological order of merit and the one obtained by averaging the group judgments of my collaborators is high, **.61 (P. E., .082)**. The most consistently minute hands of the group seem written by psychologists who concentrate by preference on details rather than principles. There are, however, a few large hands in which size is overweighted by other symptoms of care for detail. This outcome of the experiment is of very great interest in connection with our previous query whether small writing as such is evidence of general inhibitory tendencies. It indicates an affirmative answer. Certainly the strongly hyperkinetic hands emanate from psychologists who are more definitely interested in general theories than in detailed criticism or prolonged experimentation. The blurring of letters in the hyperkinetic hand and the occasional trailing off of the miniscules should not be confused with the even, clear-cut minuteness of the hand which is characterized above.

When we refer to Table VI, we find that there was complete agreement in the graphological and characterological grouping fourteen times out of a possible twenty-nine (including in this total the three half-step displacements). The percentage of successful graphological placements is 48.2 as against a possible 20 per cent. chance success. Furthermore, there are thirteen displacements of only one step. A shift from Group 1 to Group 2 is less serious than one from Group 2 to Group 3 or from Group 3 to Group 4. There are two displacements, for specimens 16 and 27, which indicate decided disagreement between the graphological and characterological judgment. Both are large, uneven, excitable hands. Probably both represent real contradiction of the graphological position, although the very extreme variation on the characterological rating of 16 should be noted. The placement of this psychologist by ten collaborators was as follows: Group I (2); Group II (3); Group III (2); Group IV (1); Group V (2).

2. *Size and Emphasis of Capitals; Feeling of Self-Worth.*

On the characterological side a five-fold grouping was asked for: (1) Strong Feeling of Self-Worth; (2) Moderated Feeling of Self-Worth; (3) Average Feeling of Self-Worth; (4) Modest Estimate of Self; (5) Excessive Modesty.

The graphological arrangement was made on the basis of size, emphasis, and ornamentation of capitals. In general, such characteristics as increased size, emphasis, and ornamentation are explained as dependent upon the heightened consciousness with which the capital is made. A detachment of a capital from the following small letter and its production by a slow drawing movement is also evidence of augmented consciousness. The increase in size with increase in feeling of self-worth is explained (1) as a specific instance of feeling for spatial relationship which correlates size with prestige and (2) as a general outcome of effort, striving, ambition. Subsidiary to size and emphasis of capitals comes graphic size in general, involving small as well as large letters.

In making my arrangement I first measured in millimeters the capitals of each specimen and then measured the average one-space letter; I also found the relative height of capital and one-space letters. I then recorded observations on the ornamentation, detachment, and design of the capital letters, in this instance examining with special care the autograph as in the autograph we find such features accentuated, and, sometimes, striking variations introduced. In this connection it should be recalled that the utilization of relative height of size of capital and one-space letter in a given collection of specimens is of doubtful value in view of the fact that the penmen may use writing systems in which the standard proportion varies considerably. One who has been taught a Spencerian system would for this very reason show a greater difference between capital and one-space letters than one who has learned a vertical system.

The correlation between the graphological arrangement and the average character rating was inconclusive; .24 (P. E., .12). There are some remarkable agreements, particularly at the beginning and end of the two orders, but five very great displacements. One of these big displacements occurs for specimen 2, already cited as an inadequate representative. Of the other four, two hands (8 and 4) exhibit, it would seem, a deceptive appearance of ultra-modesty; while two others (28 and 24) give, falsely, an impression of great self-complacency. The characterological rating is, however, a difficult one to handle. There are many different kinds of self-feeling which manifest themselves in such different ways as to make various impressions on one's acquaintances. For example, pride sensitized by self-centeredness might impress one less vigorously than a more candid and less self-conscious demeanor.

Table VI indicates that there were only six instances of identical grouping by the two methods; twelve cases where a one-step displacement occurred; and twelve cases of still greater displacement. The percentage of complete agreement is no higher than might have been anticipated by chance. Actually, it is more significant than a chance agreement as revealed by the graphological order of merit and the order made on the basis of the average characterological rating. To illustrate, No. 23 is first in the graphological order and first in the characterological, ((Group I (8); Group II (1)); No. 26 is third in the graphological arrangement and second in the characterological, ((Group I (5); Group II(2)); No. 7 is fifth in the graphological order and third in the characterological, ((Group I (6); Group II (3); Group III (2)). The agreement between the graphological and characteological rating is much more noticeable at the upper than at the lower end. Of the seven specimens placed in Group I in the characterological column three were identified by a graphological analysis but not one of those placed in Group 4 or 4.5 was selected by the graphological procedure. Certainly, there is nothing in specimens 10 or 20 that would lead to expectation of less than average feeling of self-worth. But a closer study of 6, on the basis of more material, has convinced me of error in placing it.

Curiously, this group as a whole contains more individuals who are characterized as possessing a strong feeling of self-worth than those cited as excessively modest. A professional graphologist might by utilization of the whole graphological portrait have achieved greater success than I was able to do in this limited application of a specific principle; obviously, I would have been in very considerable error in about two-fifths of my readings. On the other hand, I would have had some brilliant successes to balance my failures!

3. *Graphic Continuity; Originality of Mind versus Power of Organization.*

From our previous discussion of graphic continuity it is evident that the graphological interpretation of this element is both ambiguous and uncertain. Briefly, connected script would seem to be the product of the practical organizing type of mind; broken script of the intuitive, original, fertile type. No psychological reason for such interpretation is attempted, and, as in every other case, multiplicity of causes for the same effect is recognized.

In face of the somewhat bewildering disagreements in the traditional literature I decided to confine myself to Preyer's interpretation and with his five-fold scheme in mind (see chapter iv) I turned to my collection of hands to attempt, if possible, an arrangement into classes on the basis of degree of connectedness or disconnectedness. I tabulated for each specimen and for a constant number of words the number of breaks between letters of the same word and also the number of run-on words and the tying together by "t's." From this tabulation I made my grouping. It was, however, necessary to consider in tabulation of breaks that certain ones were much more significant than others. For example, a break between a capital letter and a following small one is less significant than a break between the small letters of the same words, largely because of the design of the capital and its production by a separate impulse of attention.

My study of my collection revealed no sample of extreme disconnection. It was possible, however, to make five groups, as follows: (1) Numerous isolated letters and breaks in letters; (2) Isolated groups of letters; (3) Occasional breaks; (4) Highly connected hands, with (a) unattached capitals; (b) attached capitals; (5) Completely connected hands with words tied together. The margin of difference between these groups was, however, very slight and after consideration I threw together the last two groups. Personally I felt that the three hands thrown originally into group 5 (namely, specimens 18, 22, and 23) represented a very different form of motor impulse from that of group 4. They engender a feeling of breathless precipitancy rather than one of smooth expertness, and had I followed my personal feeling would have been grouped with 1 rather than 4.

Reverting now to Preyer, it was evident that his classification could be applied to the present collection only in a modified form. His first class and possibly his second class were not represented at all. My first division appeared to correspond to his third; my second division to his sub-group under three. This latter division I eventually numbered 1; my first group I re-numbered 2; my third and fourth groups remained as before. From the characterological side the interpretation was as follows: (1) Original and fertile-minded, little judgment or power of organization; (2) Original and fertile-minded plus power of judgment; (3) Logical type; combinative activity; (4) Assimilative capacity, utilization of the ideas of others, neither critical nor ingenious. As a scheme for logical classification the above is far from satisfactory. As one of my collaborators wrote me in protest, the divisions are not mutually exclusive. Personally I felt the whole interpretation somewhat absurd, and my tabulation on the basis of breaks highly fantastic.

Because of the small margin of differences it did not seem feasible to make an order of merit as I had in the preceding cases. In preliminary comparison it seemed probable that two groups would be sufficient to mark the real distinction in degree of connectedness. This two-fold division could be achieved by throwing together the first two and the last two divisions. Those psychologists included in the first group would be characterized by the predominance of originality; those in the second by predominance of organizing, critical and logical capacity.

Utilizing this twofold classification I found the returns from my questionnaire interesting, and, in the light of my scepticism, unexpected. From seven to eleven judgments were passed upon 29 names of my list and in 20 of the 29 cases there was a preponderance of judgments in favor of the graphological rating, 68.9 per cent of coincidence. For example, specimen No. 27, graphologically in the second group of the twofold division, is placed by five judges in group 3, by two judges in group 4, and by one judge in group 1. Specimen No. 19 of the first graphological group is placed by five judges in group 1, by four in group 2, and in group 4 by one judge. Nine of the judges consider the penman original and fertile-minded rather than logical. Two of the big discrepancies are found among the three specimens that I placed at first in a fifth group by themselves and included finally in group 4 with an inner protest.

This comparison of the graphological and characterological rating is too crude to be satisfactory. We may, therefore, turn to the tabulation of the fourfold grouping for more complete returns. It will be observed that my collaborators were very chary in utilization of the fourth group but had found more use than I had for Group 1. In fact I had placed but one specimen in this group and, unfortunately, received too few judgments on this psychologist to justify using them. The tabulation indicates for the thirty hands used a practical agreement on fourteen specimens, or 46.6 per cent of success as against a twenty-five per cent chance agreement. There are twelve one-step displacements and four greater displacements. A shift from Group 2 to Group 3 or the reverse represents considerable error but a shift in either direction for Groups 1 and 2 is not serious. The most noticeable error is in placing 23, of which I have already spoken. Probably in balancing all traits, as would be done in a professional reading, this error would have been avoided.

The outcome of this part of the experiment is as interesting as it was unexpected. It points to a problem which should be investigated with care, namely, the possible correlation of certain types of attention with both mental and graphic traits. Of course, as always in this investigation, we are confronted with a multiplicity of causes for the effect under consideration, but in the present collection graphic discontinuity can scarcely be attributed to inexpertness since all the penmen are experienced writers although not all are expert penmen.

4. *Line Quality; Aggressiveness.*

Graphologists usually associate will-qualities with forceful stroke or heavy pressure. As accessory signs they list angularity, verticality and amplitude of writing, and the so-called dagger-stroke, evident in the terminal stroke or the bar of the "t."

My fourth grouping was made on this basis to correspond with the five divisions previously given, in a series graded from great aggressiveness to passivity. The correlational coefficient was too low to be significant, **.23 (P. E., .13)**, Two big displacements occur from one extreme in the graphological arrangement to the other extreme in the characterological, (**Nos. 8 and 26**). Omitting these two names we get a correlation coefficient of **.51 (P. E., .11)**, which is high enough to have suggestive value. The omission of the specimens indicated is, of course, illegitimate, for both exhibit real contradictions to the graphological contention. Both are unusually light tracings. We may, however, recall in this connection that there is a big margin of error in attempting to estimate pressure by the eye.

The tabular summary of groups shows ten agreements (inclusive of half-step displacements) or 33.3 per cent coincidence as against a 20 per cent chance agreement. There are thirteen one-step displacements and seven greater displacements. A one-place shift is not serious in this connection as the groups shade into one another. A character reading on this basis would give about three successes out of every four trials. The seven outstanding cases furnish material for considerable analysis of details into which, however, it is not profitable to go at present. The greatest difficulty, I suspect, lies in discriminating between the merely explosive hand and the hand which is both explosive and aggressive. Probably a similar difficulty would be encountered in choosing the decisive character trait.

5. *Slant and Alignment; Temperament.*

The graphic elements that are correlated with emotional and temperamental capacities include slant and alignment on the ground that both are akin to movements of advance or withdrawal as manifested in emotional expression in general; the eccentric or centrifugal movement is correlated with the pleasurable and the concentric or centripetal movement with unpleasant feelings. The scheme utilized by the graphologists would then be somewhat as follows: Degree of emotivity would be evidenced by degree of slant and by its variability, while the direction which this emotivity would take would be determined by the alignment; up-alignment, optimism; down-alignment, depression; fluctuating alignment, variability. A few other signs of excitability and variability might also be taken into consideration; the presence, for example, of excess movements and general signs of variability such as fluctuations in size. Moreover, large size itself is sometimes cited as symptomatic of hopefulness; reduced dimensions, of depression. The characterological grouping was as follows: (1) Optimistic, hopeful, enterprising; (2) Cheerful, active; (3) Equable, evenly active; (4) Moody, variable, fluctuating attitude toward work; (5) Pessimistic philosophy.

Preliminary to my arrangement of my collection I measured the average slant of each graphic specimen and estimated the degree of slant variability. I then listed the mannerisms of alignment, including not only the divergence of the line itself from the horizontal but such alignment as characterized the t-bar, since, according to Preyer, the manner of crossing the "t" with an up or down or straight stroke is but a special instance of alignment in general. I then selected for my midgroup—the equable in temperament—the producers of hands of slight and uniform slant, with straight and uniform alignment and general evenness and calmness of script. This classification was not difficult except for two specimens which combined minute size and vertical slant, (**3 and 22**). I next sorted out the hands that showed greater extremes and variability in slant, grading these with respect both to degree of slant and of variability and separating into two groups on the basis of up or down alignment. Sub-division of these groups was made on the basis of degree of slant and of variability, but weight was also given to size in separating Groups 1 and 2 and in Group 4 (Moody) were included cases of fluctuating alignment, particularly the line convex or concave in form. Group 5 included hands with a perceptible down-alignment. I then arranged the names within each group seriatim. Cases of fluctuating alignment in combination with extreme slant were most difficult to place and in a number of instances my notes indicate a wavering in decision between Groups 1 and 4, with final uncertainty as to proper placement.

Slant and alignment as a basis of classification involve great chance for error inasmuch as both are especially variable. In making such observations as the above, one should have at hand a number of specimens of a given hand, which was not the case in this investigation except for a few penmen. In addition, there are the usual difficulties arising from difference in system of writing utilized; a vertical system encouraging a less degree of slant than the Spencerian. It should, however, be observed that the slant in the specimens of the present collection is extreme in only a very few instances. A tendency to back-slant is perceivable in but a few specimens and then only in spots. I have stated elsewhere my conviction that such a tendency is related to latent ambidextrality, a point which would have no connection whatever with temperamental traits unless possibly the more highly unidextrous person is more objective-minded and, in consequence, more cheerful and hopeful in temperament than the ambidextral type, an hypothesis highly speculative but in harmony with a number of observations which I have gathered. The present collection yielded only one specimen of complete backhand writing and unfortunately too few of my collaborators were acquainted with this individual to make possible a characterization of him.

It was evident that my collaborators found great difficulty in arranging in temperamental groups the names sent them. Considerable personal acquaintance is necessary before one can confidently risk such a judgment. Just as I experienced uncertainty in separating Groups 1 and 2, so too did certain of my collaborators, indicating this by linking the two groups. Although the groups do not give satisfactory basis for an order of merit, I have attempted such a serial arrangement as a possible way of bringing the records together.

The correlation between the graphological and characterological arrangement (**.27, P. E., .12**) is too low to be significant. Study of the serial arrangements indicates, however, an agreement on one-third of the twenty-seven names. A big discrepancy occurs for specimen 19, placed graphologically in Group 4 but with a question mark, as possibly belonging in 1 or 2. Seven of nine judges placed 19 in either the first or second group so that the evidence of moodiness would seem deceptive. Specimen 4, placed by the average judgment well up toward the cheerful end of the spectrum, exhibits, graphologically speaking, every sign of a moody, fluctuating disposition. Five judges place 4 in Group 1; one in Group 2; and three in Group 4. Among these latter judges is the individual who probably knows 4 most intimately. Group 5 was very sparingly used by my collaborators and the graphological arrangement included only three names in this group. Only in one of these three cases is the graphological rating in harmony with the average judgment. No. 17 is of especial interest in this connection. It presents an extraordinary fall in alignment, a characteristic which I have noted in a number of specimens of writing by this same penman. I have a feeling—but without specific information to back it—that this hand presents pathological features; it may be conditioned by defective vision or general motor incoordination. Following the graphological tradition I placed it in Group 5, but in this case the falling alignment is not significant of a pessimistic outlook as evidenced by the general agreement as to the writer's cheerful or at least equable disposition.

The tabulation of the results by groups shows a complete agreement on only six names, scarcely more than might be expected by a chance arrangement. In two other cases the results are indecisive. There are nine one-step displacements; ten displacements of more than one step. The tabulation reveals in a number of instances very great discrepancy in temperamental judgments as given by my collaborators. No other arrangement gave so many extreme variations. For specimens 4, 5, 8, 18, and 26 the variation is so extreme as to lead one to have as much confidence in the graphological as in the personal rating.

6. *Explosive and Inhibited Make-Up.*

In testing the possibility of deducing from handwriting explosive or inhibited tendencies, I turned from the more conventional treatments in the usual treatises and adopted Klages' scheme for determination of the degree to which psychic energy is freely liberated or the reverse. The general conception reminds us somewhat of James' description of the obstructed and explosive types of will. We have here, I suspect, the central problem in utilization of handwriting in psychodiagnosis, just as we have many indications that the distinction so well phrased by James is an essential one, particularly if we recognize that an explosive type of will may result either from defective inhibition or exaggerated impulsion and an obstructed one from excessive inhibition or insufficient impulsion.

Klages bases his scheme for identification of the free and retarded hand on the results of experiments upon disguised handwriting. The graphic characteristics that are accentuated when control is at a maximum become then symptomatic of a hand, the writer of which is highly self-conscious and maintains a high degree of control without yielding to

The graphological arrangement was made on the basis of size, emphasis, and ornamentation of capitals. In general, such characteristics as increased size, emphasis, and ornamentation are explained as dependent upon the heightened consciousness with which the capital is made. A detachment of a capital from the following small letter and its production by a slow drawing movement is also evidence of augmented consciousness. The increase in size with increase in feeling of self-worth is explained (1) as a specific instance of feeling for spatial relationship which correlates size with prestige and (2) as a general outcome of effort, striving, ambition. Subsidiary to size and emphasis of capitals comes graphic size in general, involving small as well as large letters.

In making my arrangement I first measured in millimeters the capitals of each specimen and then measured the average one-space letter; I also found the relative height of capital and one-space letters. I then recorded observations on the ornamentation, detachment, and design of the capital letters, in this instance examining with special care the autograph as in the autograph we find such features accentuated, and, sometimes, striking variations introduced. In this connection it should be recalled that the utilization of relative height of size of capital and one-space letter in a given collection of specimens is of doubtful value in view of the fact that the penmen may use writing systems in which the standard proportion varies considerably. One who has been taught a Spencerian system would for this very reason show a greater difference between capital and one-space letters than one who has learned a vertical system.

The correlation between the graphological arrangement and the average character rating was inconclusive; .24 (P. E., .12). There are some remarkable agreements, particularly at the beginning and end of the two orders, but five very great displacements. One of these big displacements occurs for specimen 2, already cited as an inadequate representative. Of the other four, two hands (8 and 4) exhibit, it would seem, a deceptive appearance of ultra-modesty; while two others (28 and 24) give, falsely, an impression of great self-complacency. The characterological rating is, however, a difficult one to handle. There are many different kinds of self-feeling which manifest themselves in such different ways as to make various impressions on one's acquaintances. For example, pride sensitized by self-centeredness might impress one less vigorously than a more candid and less self-conscious demeanor.

Table VI indicates that there were only six instances of identical grouping by the two methods; twelve cases where a one-step displacement occurred; and twelve cases of still greater displacement. The percentage of complete agreement is no higher than might have been anticipated by chance. Actually, it is more significant than a chance agreement as revealed by the graphological order of merit and the order made on the basis of the average characterological rating. To illustrate, No. 23 is first in the graphological order and first in the characterological, ((Group I (8); Group II (1)); No. 26 is third in the graphological arrangement and second in the characterological, ((Group I (5); Group II(2)); No. 7 is fifth in the graphological order and third in the characterological, ((Group I (6); Group II (3); Group III (2)). The agreement between the graphological and characteological rating is much more noticeable at the upper than at the lower end. Of the seven specimens placed in Group I in the characterological column three were identified by a graphological analysis but not one of those placed in Group 4 or 4.5 was selected by the graphological procedure. Certainly, there is nothing in specimens 10 or 20 that would lead to expectation of less than average feeling of self-worth. But a closer study of 6, on the basis of more material, has convinced me of error in placing it.

Curiously, this group as a whole contains more individuals who are characterized as possessing a strong feeling of self-worth than those cited as excessively modest. A professional graphologist might by utilization of the whole graphological portrait have achieved greater success than I was able to do in this limited application of a specific principle; obviously, I would have been in very considerable error in about two-fifths of my readings. On the other hand, I would have had some brilliant successes to balance my failures!

3. *Graphic Continuity; Originality of Mind versus Power of Organization.*

From our previous discussion of graphic continuity it is evident that the graphological interpretation of this element is both ambiguous and uncertain. Briefly, connected script would seem to be the product of the practical organizing type of mind; broken script of the intuitive, original, fertile type. No psychological reason for such interpretation is attempted, and, as in every other case, multiplicity of causes for the same effect is recognized.

In face of the somewhat bewildering disagreements in the traditional literature I decided to confine myself to Preyer's interpretation and with his five-fold scheme in mind (see chapter iv) I turned to my collection of hands to attempt, if possible, an arrangement into classes on the basis of degree of connectedness or disconnectedness. I tabulated for each specimen and for a constant number of words the number of breaks between letters of the same word and also the number of run-on words and the tying together by "t's." From this tabulation I made my grouping. It was, however, necessary to consider in tabulation of breaks that certain ones were much more significant than others. For example, a break between a capital letter and a following small one is less significant than a break between the small letters of the same words, largely because of the design of the capital and its production by a separate impulse of attention.

My study of my collection revealed no sample of extreme disconnection. It was possible, however, to make five groups, as follows: (1) Numerous isolated letters and breaks in letters; (2) Isolated groups of letters; (3) Occasional breaks; (4) Highly connected hands, with (a) unattached capitals; (b) attached capitals; (5) Completely connected hands with words tied together. The margin of difference between these groups was, however, very slight and after consideration I threw together the last two groups. Personally I felt that the three hands thrown originally into group 5 (namely, specimens 18, 22, and 23) represented a very different form of motor impulse from that of group 4. They engender a feeling of breathless precipitancy rather than one of smooth expertness, and had I followed my personal feeling would have been grouped with 1 rather than 4.

Reverting now to Preyer, it was evident that his classification could be applied to the present collection only in a modified form. His first class and possibly his second class were not represented at all. My first division appeared to correspond to his third; my second division to his sub-group under three. This latter division I eventually numbered 1; my first group I re-numbered 2; my third and fourth groups remained as before. From the characterological side the interpretation was as follows: (1) Original and fertile-minded, little judgment or power of organization; (2) Original and fertile-minded plus power of judgment; (3) Logical type; combinative activity; (4) Assimilative capacity, utilization of the ideas of others, neither critical nor ingenious. As a scheme for logical classification the above is far from satisfactory. As one of my collaborators wrote me in protest, the divisions are not mutually exclusive. Personally I felt the whole interpretation somewhat absurd, and my tabulation on the basis of breaks highly fantastic.

Because of the small margin of differences it did not seem feasible to make an order of merit as I had in the preceding cases. In preliminary comparison it seemed probable that two groups would be sufficient to mark the real distinction in degree of connectedness. This two-fold division could be achieved by throwing together the first two and the last two divisions. Those psychologists included in the first group would be characterized by the predominance of originality; those in the second by predominance of organizing, critical and logical capacity.

Utilizing this twofold classification I found the returns from my questionnaire interesting, and, in the light of my scepticism, unexpected. From seven to eleven judgments were passed upon 29 names of my list and in 20 of the 29 cases there was a preponderance of judgments in favor of the graphological rating, 68.9 per cent of coincidence. For example, specimen No. 27, graphologically in the second group of the twofold division, is placed by five judges in group 3, by two judges in group 4, and by one judge in group 1. Specimen No. 19 of the first graphological group is placed by five judges in group 1, by four in group 2, and in group 4 by one judge. Nine of the judges consider the penman original and fertile-minded rather than logical. Two of the big discrepancies are found among the three specimens that I placed at first in a fifth group by themselves and included finally in group 4 with an inner protest.

This comparison of the graphological and characterological rating is too crude to be satisfactory. We may, therefore, turn to the tabulation of the fourfold grouping for more complete returns. It will be observed that my collaborators were very chary in utilization of the fourth group but had found more use than I had for Group 1. In fact I had placed but one specimen in this group and, unfortunately, received too few judgments on this psychologist to justify using them. The tabulation indicates for the thirty hands used a practical agreement on fourteen specimens, or 46.6 per cent of success as against a twenty-five per cent chance agreement. There are twelve one-step displacements and four greater displacements. A shift from Group 2 to Group 3 or the reverse represents considerable error but a shift in either direction for Groups 1 and 2 is not serious. The most noticeable error is in placing 23, of which I have already spoken. Probably in balancing all traits, as would be done in a professional reading, this error would have been avoided.

The outcome of this part of the experiment is as interesting as it was unexpected. It points to a problem which should be investigated with care, namely, the possible correlation of certain types of attention with both mental and graphic traits. Of course, as always in this investigation, we are confronted with a multiplicity of causes for the effect under consideration, but in the present collection graphic discontinuity can scarcely be attributed to inexpertness since all the penmen are experienced writers although not all are expert penmen.

4. *Line Quality; Aggressiveness.*

Graphologists usually associate will-qualities with forceful stroke or heavy pressure. As accessory signs they list angularity, verticality and amplitude of writing, and the so-called dagger-stroke, evident in the terminal stroke or the bar of the "t."

My fourth grouping was made on this basis to correspond with the five divisions previously given, in a series graded from great aggressiveness to passivity. The correlational coefficient was too low to be significant, **.23 (P. E., .13).**

Two big displacements occur from one extreme in the graphological arrangement to the other extreme in the characterological, (**Nos. 8 and 26**). Omitting these two names we get a correlation coefficient of **.51 (P. E., .11)**, which is high enough to have suggestive value. The omission of the specimens indicated is, of course, illegitimate, for both exhibit real contradictions to the graphological contention. Both are unusually light tracings. We may, however, recall in this connection that there is a big margin of error in attempting to estimate pressure by the eye.

The tabular summary of groups shows ten agreements (inclusive of half-step displacements) or 33.3 per cent coincidence as against a 20 per cent chance agreement. There are thirteen one-step displacements and seven greater displacements. A one-place shift is not serious in this connection as the groups shade into one another. A character reading on this basis would give about three successes out of every four trials. The seven outstanding cases furnish material for considerable analysis of details into which, however, it is not profitable to go at present. The greatest excitement. Two other hands of the collection show pathological signs. One exhibits a fine tremor very evident under the microscope and the other presents an extraordinary fall in alignment.

TABLE VI Graphological and Characterological Judgment

Specimen	I Graphol rating	I Character rating	I M. V.	II Graphol rating	II Character rating	II M. V.	III Graphol rating	III Character rating	III M. V.	IV Graphol rating	IV Character rating	IV M. V.	V Graphol rating	V Character rating	V M. V.	VI Graphol rating	VI Character rating	VI M. V.	Av. M. V.
1	2	2	.40	3	3	.57	4	4	.32	5	3	.50	1	3	.17	3	3	.65	.44
2	4	3	.50	1	3	.72	4	2	.22	2	3	.45	4	3	.29	2	3	.29	.41
3	1	2	.67	3	2	.65	3	3	.72	3	2	.45	3?	3.5	.65	4	4	.61	.63
4	4	3	.22	5	1	.70	3	2	.22	1	1	.30	4	1	1.11	3	2	.45	.50
5	4	3	.61	3	2	.50	2	3	.39	2	3	.80	3	2	1.11	5	3	.33	.62
6	4	3	.44	3	4	.70	3	3	.28	1	4	.50	3	3	.50	2	3	1.56	.66
7	3	3	.60	1	1	.64	2	2	.18	1	1	.35	4?	2 } 4 }	. . . .	5	2	.70	
8	3	3	.60	3	2	.40	2	2	.27	4	1	.30	1	1	1.25	3	2	.50	.55
9	1	.	. .	4	2	.20	2	2.5	.83	3	3	.20	.	.	. .	4	.	. .	
10	2	3	.20	3	4.5	.70	3	2	.44	3	4	.11	2	3	.44	2	4	.60	.42
11	4	3	.10	5	3	.80	3	2	.44	2	3	.72	4	3	.56	5	3	.55	.53
12	4	3	.25	4	3	.38	3	3	.33	4	3	.28	.	.	. .	.	.	. .	
13	1	2	.44	5	3	.56	4	3	.50	3	4	.70	4	2	.50	4	3.5	.64	.56
14	2	2	.86	1	3	.56	4	4	1.20	2	2	.56	1	2.5	1.00	2	3	.43	.77
15	4	3	.56	4	3	.63	2	3	.57	2	4	.63	4	3	.33	5	3.5	.50	.54
16	5	2.	1.10	2	1	.81	2	2	.80	1	1	.90	4	2 } 4 }	. . . .	1	3	.94	
17	4	4	.93	4	3	.90	4	4	1.10	3	3.5	.594	5	3	.63	4	3	.50	.78
18	3	3	.50	1	2	.53	4	3	.70	3	2	.22	5?	1	1.33	2	2	.40	.61
19	5	4.5	.67	2	1	.90	2	1	.60	2	2	.60	4?	1	.99	2	1	.65	.74
20	2	2	.88	2	4	.90	4	3	.50	2	3	.60	1	3	.75	3	3	.50	.69
21	2	2	.14	2	3.5	.50	4	3	1.00	4	4	.84	2	.	. .	3	3.5	.50	
22	3	3	.70	2	1	.90	4	3	.63	1	2.5	.70	3	3	.89	3	2	.45	.71
23	4	4.5	.99	1	1	.11	4	1	.33	1	2	.38	1	1	.11	1	1	.21	.36
24	4	3	.67	1	2.5	.83	3	3	.29	2	3	.25	4	3	.85	1	3	.71	.60
25	4	4	.70	1	3	.64	4	2.5	.61	4	2	.40	1	2	.56	2	3	.13	.51
26	5	4.5	.43	1	1	.25	2	2	.63	4	1	.44	4	1	1.25	1	2	.50	.58
27	4	2.5	.43	2	2	.60	4	3	.50	2	3	.50	4	3	.50	3	3	.71	.54
28	2	3	.44	1	3	.60	4	3	.33	3	2.5	.50	2	3.5	.61	2	3	.55	.51
29	3	3	.22	2	3	.33	2	2	.56	3	3	.30	2	2	.62	3	3	.14	.36
30	3	4	.50	3	3	.69	2	2	.75	1	2	.69	5	4	.14	5	3	.89	.61

CHAPTER IX

SUMMARY AND CONCLUSIONS

We are now ready to venture upon a few concluding remarks with reference to certain problems suggested in the introductory chapter:

(1) The specific results of, and program for, investigation precipitated by graphological discussions, and

(2) The possibility of utilizing graphic products in diagnostic tests.

(1) To recapitulate briefly. We have found reason to believe that graphic size is symptomatic of the free release of energy or the reverse and that extreme variation from conventional standards has evidential value in an inter-group comparison as well as in intra-individual comparison. We have found that a high degree of variability in size, slant, alignment, and similar graphic elements, witnesses lack of mastery of the motor impulse by reason of defective control or excessive impetuosity, and that there is reason to believe that such extreme variability is evidence of the possession of specific mental traits. Effortful control of graphic movements likewise introduces very definite signs. We have found reason to correlate frequent breaks in graphic continuity in an experienced hand with speculative interests, and the contrasting hand with practicality. On the other hand, we have encountered a stumbling block in our attempt to utilize slant and alignment in temperamental diagnosis. Even here, however, indications were not wanting of some curious confirmations of the graphological position. Such indication, for example, is found in the correlative changes that occurred with shifts in mood for Subject II in the investigation on individual variability, and in the curious similarity between type of slant and expressive attitude which the experiment on graphic individuality revealed in a number of cases. The concept of the explosive versus the inhibited

hand proved particularly enlightening although the limitation of graphic expression by conventional standards greatly embarrasses interpretation of symptoms.

Furthermore, the records from study of a given collection of hands suggest that certain very specific psychodiagnostic correlations deserve respectful consideration. Our percentages of successes compared very favorably with those obtained by Binet in his investigation in spite of the fact that we were dealing with specific rather than general correlations, with a very limited range of material, and were obliged to dispense with the services of the expert graphologist.

The detailed report of our employment of handwriting in psychodiagnosis should be compared with Hollingsworth's investigation of the worth of judgments of character based upon study of a photograph. (**24:41 f.**). Limiting ourselves to the records made by the individual judges in Hollingworth's test (see page 52) we find that our one amateur graphologist was, on the whole, rather more uniformly successful. But the traits on which judgments were passed were not, of course, directly comparable. It is rather interesting in this connection to note that in the case of the one trait where a comparison may be instituted, namely, the average estimation of "Conceit" from the photograph and of "Feeling of Self-Worth" from handwriting, the second source of information was slightly more accurate. All this by the way.

Chiefly, our results are of value in that they outline a program for further investigation. They witness the need of more precise analysis of graphic elements and the influence upon each of varying degrees of impulsion and of inhibition. Another suggested problem is the relation of certain types of attention to the smoothness or interruption of the motor impulse. We have found some curious problems inherent in back-slant; the causes that determine it should be investigated. A genetic study of the development of individuality in hands should be undertaken, and, also, the tracing of similarity in the specific characteristics of family chirography.

(2) The attempt to utilize graphic products in diagnostic tests involves, as a preliminary, scrutiny of possible classification of mental types. A number of simple bipartite classifications which are current in psychological texts bear obvious implication of a pattern fundamentally motor in origin. The particular categories we have in mind have been cited frequently in the preceding chapters. They include the following organization of types: Explosive or Obstructed; Sensory or Motor; Hyperkinetic or Hypokinetic (akinetic). Another distinction is rapidly becoming widely accepted, namely, the division into an introverted or an extroverted disposition. Although the angle of approach is in this instance very different, the division itself effects a very similar grouping of individuals and hence raises again the question as to the relationship of motor impulses to these psychic patterns, a question which suggests a method of experimental attack of certain modern theories which up to the present have been presented largely in dogmatic form.

With reference to the other organizations of types we may say a few words. James' classic description of the explosive and obstructed will has been appealed to in our experimental sections. Certainly the varieties of reaction characterized by him under the above terms have been found most enlightening in our everyday comprehension of character, including as they do the two forms of explosive will because of either exaggerated impulsion or defective inhibition, and the two forms of obstructed will, because of either insufficient impulsion or excessive inhibition. Naturally one expects to meet extreme types but rarely and one recognizes the fact that emotional excitement may change the inhibited individual into the explosive or that age may transform the explosive person into the inhibited. Moreover, many individuals appear to fluctuate from one type to the other more or less periodically.

Much that is said of the explosive-obstructed make-up is very general in nature and not subject to experimental analysis. Davenport's recent attempt to study the inheritance of temperamental patterns and his conclusion that defective inhibition of the nomadic instinct is "probably a sex-linked, recessive, monohybrid trait" opens out the way for a new method of study of mental types, although his study of the more complex temperamental patterns serves to emphasize the obstacles that must be overcome.

The division into sensory-motor types was first made in connection with reaction experiments. Now is not the time to rehearse the varieties in interpretation of the outcome of such experiments, nor the development of precision in analysis. It would be venturesome in the extreme to attempt to formulate any simple conclusions as to reaction-times and temperamental patterns. We may, however, utilize the terms sensory and motor in a purely descriptive way and with Baldwin (**2:163** f.) characterize the active or motile person as very responsive to suggestion. "He tends to act promptly, quickly, unreflectively—generally such a person, child or adult, is said to jump at conclusions—Psychologically such a person is dominated by Habit." He is domineering and self-assertive; the man of action. The "sensory child is passive, more troubled by physical inertia, more contemplative when a little older, less apt in learning to act out new movements, less quick at taking a hint." The sensory individual is the observer, the thinker; he is non-suggestible, non-expressive, non-self-revealing. Any simple registration of such contrasting traits in a motor reaction would be of greatest service in character analysis.

Hirt believes that there is a natural form of reaction determined by inborn constitution. Moreover, his experiments on writing have convinced him of a motor and sensorial writing-type. The penmen who belong to the first type make writing-movements; those who belong to the second draw "graphic signs." But is this motor or sensorial character of writing a significant trait? And what proof have we that differing psychophysical personalities are mirrored in these reaction types? Hirt appears to assume the truth of this latter proposition but he adds that an individual of one type may in a particular activity belong to a contrasting type. So writing-type constitutes only *one* symptom out of many possible symptoms. The motor reaction is the more rapid, energetic, and emphatic; the sensorial more heavily slow and controlled.

The third distinction to which we referred, namely, hyperkinetic or hypokinetic (akinetic) types is an outcome of study of neuropathic or psychopathic constitutions. Of this distinction Southard (**44**) writes: "In confronting instances of over- or under-activity, the analytical student should consider in turn whether his given example of hyperkinesis is hyperkinesis by defect or by excess; and the same process is of value in the analysis of akinetic phenomena."

Hirt observes that the manic and depressive make-ups exhibit parallelism in psychic and in expressive activities and lists self-confidence, indiscretion, mental energy, hasty, unmotived and rapid acts as characteristic of the first; retardation, indecision, anxiety, lack of self-confidence and inactivity as characteristic of the second. From overt expression one draws conclusions concerning the mental make-up.

In the study of temperamental organization, utilization of some form of motor expression should, therefore, prove of great value if it were possible to disentangle the characterological phases from those impressed upon the movement by pressure of the environment. Handwriting suggests itself as more convenient to utilize than manner of walk, gesture, or emotional expression because of the fact that it produces a record which can be utilized for repeated observation. It is manifestly of great complexity and subject to great environmental pressure, but in this respect it certainly presents no more difficulties than do other forms of expression. And it would seem more simply susceptible of analysis than is posture or walk or gesture.

Our preceding study has revealed distinctions in hands thoroughly in line with the theoretical categories listed above. But granting the existence of explosive and inhibited hands, of motor and sensory writing, of hyperkinetic and hypokinetic chirography, what guarantee have we that they point beyond themselves to a general motor make-up. Can any specific motor pattern lead to inference of a general temperamental pattern? Do not habit and training cause strange inconsistencies in expression; fluency, for example, in speech but halting gesture?

Signs of inhibition may indeed arise as an outcome of motor conflict, but how variously such conflicts may be motivated! Reverting to inhibitions in graphic movements, we have found that they may originate in shift from one system of writing to a second, in bad eyesight, in transfer from right to the left hand in writing or the reverse, or even arise from the writing material that is utilized. On the other hand, graphic smoothness or expertness or chirographic impetuosity may possibly originate in ample practice, or in thorough grounding in the best form of graphic movement. Does adequate comprehension of the multiplicity of causes for graphic effects check any tendency to diagnostic generalization? Yes, and no. It undoubtedly enforces conservatism in attitude and insistence upon experimental procedure but it does not place an impassable barrier in the way of positive interpretation of results. The foregoing account in its comparative treatment of the various methods of studying handwriting and in its experimental studies has furnished some indication of where to look for positive results, sufficient material to at least encourage a further search for a series of graphic tests which might be utilized to get insight into the type of organization of a reagent and so supplement intelligence tests. So far, of course, as these tests concern the characterization of the strength or weakness of the motor impulse, its energy or free release or retardation they would have value in giving the *form* of personality only. They would give us no information as to the direction in which those impulses would be applied, nor insight into the manifold individual differences in fundamental impulses and sensitivities which are basal to character organization.

Our further search along this line for diagnostic tests will consist not wholly in utilization of free handwriting but in such restrictions of it as arise in retarded, accelerated, disguised, and automatic writing. In the hope of reaching positive results I am now putting such tests to the proof.

REFERENCES

1. Ayers, L. P.: (a) A Scale for Measuring the Quality of Handwriting of School Children. N. Y.: Russell Sage Foundation (1912).
   (b) A Scale for Measuring Quality of Handwriting of Adults. N. Y.: Russell Sage Foundation (1915).
2. Baldwin, J. M.: The Story of the Mind. (1902).
3. Binet, A: (a) L'écriture pendant les états d'excitation. Annèe psychol., 9, (1903).
   (b) Sur le grossissement provoqué de l'écriture Archiv de psychol., 4, (1904).
   (c) Les révélations de l'écriture d'après un contrôle scientifique. (1906).
4. Bingham, W. V.: Some Norms of Dartmouth Freshman. Jour. Ed. Psy., 7, (1916).
5. Blackford, K.: Character Analysis.
6. Booth, M. H.: How to Read Character in Handwriting. A Guide for the Beginner and Student in Graphology. (1910).
7. Brown W.: The Psychology of Writing. Rep. Brit. Ass. Adv. Sci. (1913).
8. Busse, H. H.: Die Graphologie. (1895).
9. Crépieux—Jamin, J.: L'Écriture et le Caractère. (1896).
10. Davenport, C. D.: The Feebly Inhibited: Nomadism or the Wandering Impulse with a Special Reference to Heredity—Inheritance and Temperament. Carnegie Institute of Washington. (1915).
11. Dearborn, G. V. N.: (a) Kinaesthesia and the Intelligent Will. Amer. Jour. Psy., 24, (1913).
   (b) Intuition. Psy. Rev. 22, (1917).
12. Deschamps, L.: La philosophie de l'écriture. (1892.)
13. Diehl, A.: Ueber die Eigenschaften der Schrift bei Gesunden. Psychol. Arbeiten, 3, (1899).
14. Downey, J. E.: (a) Control Processes in Modified Handwriting. Psy. Rev. Monog. 37, (1908).
   (b) Preliminary Study of Family Resemblance in Handwriting. Uni. of Wyo. Dep't. of Psy. Bull. No. 1, (1910).
   (c) Judgments on the Sex of Handwriting. Psy. Rev., 17, (1910).
   (d) Judgments on Handwriting Similarity and Difference. J. of Phil., Psy. and Sci. Meth., 11, (1914).
   (e) Automatic Writing (with J. E. Anderson), Amer. Jour. of Psy., 26, (1915).

(f) Handwriting Disguise, Journal App. Psy., 1, (1917).

15. Erlenmeyer, A.: Die Schrift, Grundzuege ihrer Physiologie u. Pathologie. (1879).

16. Freeman, F. N.: (a) Preliminary Experiments on Writing Reactions. Psy. Rev. Monog., 34, (1907).
(b) Problems and Methods of Investigation in Handwriting. Jour. of Ed. Psy., 3, (1912).
(c) Experimental Analysis of the Writing Movement. Psy. Monog. 75, (1914).
(d) The Teaching of Handwriting. (1914).

17. French, W. L.: What Your Handwriting Reveals. (1914).

18. de Fursac, R.: Les Ecrits et les Dessins dans les Maladies nerveuses et mentales. (1905).

19. Gesell, A. L.: Accuracy in Handwriting as related to School Intelligence and Sex. Amer. Jour. Psy., 17, (1906).

20. Grommès, M.: Les Facteurs Musculaires du Graphism. Le Revue Psy., 6, (1913).

21 Gray, C. T.: The Training of Judgment in the Use of the Ayers Scale for Handwriting. Jour. of Ed. Psy., 6, (1915).

22. Gross, A.: Untersuchungen ueber die Schrift Gesunder und Geisteskranker. Psy. Arb., 2, (1899).

23. Hirt, E.: (a) Ueber empirisch begruendete Bewertung der normalen und pathologischen Handschrift. Arch. f. d. ges. Psy., 23, (1912).
(b) Untersuchungen ueber das Schreiben u. die Schrift. Psy. Arb., 6, (1914).

24. Hollingworth, H. L.: Vocational Psychology. (1916).

25. Holt, E. B.: The Freudian Wish. (1916).

26. Klages, L.: (a) Die Probleme der Graphologie: Entwurf einer Psychodiagnostik. (1910).
(b) Begriff und Tatbestand der Handschrift, Zsch. f. Psy., 63, (1912).

27 Koester, R.: Die Schrift bei Geisteskrankheiten. (1903).

28. Lemaitre, A.: Un Test basé sur le modification de l'écriture. Arch. de psy., 3, (1903).

29. Lomer, G.: (a) Ein Fall von zirkularer Psychose, graphologisch gewuerdigt. Zsch. f. d. ges. Neur u. Psychiat, 20, (1913).
(b) Ueber graphologische Kennzeichen des Schwachsinns. Arch. f. Psychiat, 53, (1914).

30. Mayer, M.: Ueber die Beeinflussung der Schrift durch den Alkohol. Psy. Arb., 3, (1901).

31. McAllister, C. N.: Researches on Movements Used in Handwriting. Studies from Yale Psy. Lab., 8, (1900).

32. Meumann, E.: Vorlesungen zur Einfuehrung in die Experimentelle Paedogogik und ihre psychologischen Grundlagen, 2, (1907).

33. Meyer, A., Jelliffe, S. E., Hoch, A.: Dementia Praecox. (1911).

34. Meyer, G.: (a) Ueber Schriftverstellung, Grap. Monatshefte, 4, (1900).
(b) Die wissenschaftlichen Grundlagen der Graphologie. (1901).

35. Naecke, P.: (a) Biologisches und Forensisches zur Handschrift. Neur. Centbl., 30, (1911).
(b) Einige Bemerkungen bez. der Zeichnungen und anderer Kuenstlerischer Aeusserungen von Geisteskranken. Zsch. f. d. ges. Neur. u. Psychiat, 17, (1913).

36. Osborn, A. S.: (a) Questioned Documents. A Study of questioned documents with an outline of methods by which the facts may be discovered and shown. (1910).
(b) Form Blindness or Psychology of Sight in Relation to Legal Procedure. Case and Comment, 19, (1913).
(c) Errors in Identification of Handwriting. Amer. Law. Rev., 48, (1914).

37. Pellat, S.: L'Education aidée par la Graphologie. (1906).

38. Poppée, R.: Graphologie. (1908).

39. Preyer, W.: Psychologie des Schreibens. (1895).

40. Prince, M.: The Dissociation of a Personality. (1906).

41. Schneickert, H.: (a) Graphologische Uebergriffe. Arch. f. Krim.-Anthropol. u. Kriminalistik, 39, (1910).
(b) Die neue Handschriftensammlung der Berliner Kriminalpolizei. Arch. f. Krim.-Anthropol. u. Kriminalistik, 39, (1910).

42. Schneidemuehl, G.: (a) Handschrift und Carakter. Ein Lehrrésumé of the researches and experiments Grund wissenschaftlicher und praktischer Studien. (1911).
(b) Die Psychologie der Handschrift. Neur. Centbl., 31, (1912).

43 Starch, D.: (a) Unconscious Imitation in Handwriting. Psy. Rev., 18, (1911).
(b) The Similarity of Brothers and Sister in Mental Traits. Psy. Rev., 24, (1917).

44. Southard, E. E.: General Psychopathology. Psy. Bull. 14, (1917).

45. Thompson, M. E.: Psychology and Pedagogy of Writing: a résumé of the researches and experiments bearing on the history and pedagogy of writing. (1911).

46. Thorndike, E. L.: (a) Handwriting. Teachers College Record, 11, (1910).
(b) The resemblance of young twins in handwriting. Amer. Natural., 49, (1915).
47. Woodworth, R. S.: The Accuracy of Voluntary Movement. Psy. Rev. Monog. 13, (1899).